Hikes & Walks

IN THE BERKSHIRE HILLS

Hikes &Walks

IN THE BERKSHIRE HILLS
Third Edition

LAUREN R. STEVENS

Countryman Press
Woodstock, Vermont

ISBN 978-1-58157-068-7
ISSN 1547-531X

Cover and interior design by Jane McWhorter
Cover photograph © A. Blake Gardner
Maps and illustrations by Alison Kolesar. Supplemental maps by
Vaughan Gray

Map on p. 112 is adapted from "Pittsfield: A Self-Guided
Historical Walking Tour" by Pittsfield Central.

Published by The Countryman Press, P.O. Box 748, Woodstock,
Vermont 05091

Distributed by W. W. Norton & Company, Inc., 500 Fifth Avenue,
New York, NY 10110

Printed in the United States of America

10 9 8 7 6 5 4

BERKSHIRE, THE BERKSHIRES, THE BERKSHIRE HILLS

What is the name of this place, anyway? The original Berkshire is in England, south of Oxford. There it's pronounced "Bark-shuh." "Shire" refers to an Anglo-Saxon administrative district.

Purists refer to the "Berkshire Hills," meaning specifically what this book calls the southern Taconics, including peaks in New York State. The logic of calling all hills in Berkshire County the Berkshire Hills seems to be gaining acceptance.

Berkshire residents—and visitors—refer to the area variously as "Berkshire County," as simply "Berkshire," and as "the Berkshires," actually a 20th-century term created to publicize the area. This book is similarly inconsistent.

To my parents

"Then all my gladsome way along . . ."
—Johann J. Schütz (1640–1690)

TABLE OF CONTENTS

HIKES & WALKS

SOUTH COUNTY

NORTH COUNTY

LIST OF MAPS

Maps and Page Numbers

**U.S. Geological
Survey
Quadrangle**

CENTRAL COUNTY

NORTH COUNTY

WALKS FOR THE BLIND AND DISABLED

United States Geological Survey (USGS) maps are available, by quadrangles, as listed above. These do not conform to town boundaries, but are named by the distinguishing feature on each quad. The maps are available at book and sporting goods stores (see the Appendices), www.usgs.gov, ASK USGS on line, 1-888-ASK-USGS, or from U.S. Department of Interior, USGS, Reston, VA 22092 or Denver, CO 80225.

MAP LEGEND

paved road

unpaved road

trail described in text (except where it coincides with Appalachian Trail)

Appalachian Trail

900 contour lines

river or stream

seasonally present stream

rail line

Mass. / Conn. state line

7 U.S. highway

8 State highway

90 Interstate highway

INTRODUCTION

Whether you want to amble in an afternoon through an azalea grove or take a strenuous day hike with sweeping vistas of five states, it's tough to beat Berkshire County. For variety and tradition, few areas in this country offer prospects as rich as those of the western end of Massachusetts. Some of the routes described in this book move you inward, toward contemplation and quiet. As Henry David Thoreau said of the Bellows Pipe, his trail to the summit of Mount Greylock, "It seemed a road for the pilgrim to enter upon who would climb to the gates of heaven." Other routes, perhaps beside brooks dropping for hundreds of feet or along rocky ridges fringed with fir, make you want to shout with joy. And through them all you absorb the rhythms that previous generations have trod, an at-oneness with ancients known and unknown, famous and infamous.

These descriptions overflow into neighboring states and counties because Berkshire's mountainous boundaries—the Taconics, Greens, Hoosacs, and Litchfield Hills—themselves offer prime areas to get out and enjoy the out-of-doors under your own locomotion. The Berkshire region can test the limbs and meet the curiosities of daily walkers in infinite ways. This little book is content to list many of the best: 40 walks and 17 hikes, 8 walks for the blind, together with brief descriptions of 20 towns and cities in which they mostly take place.

A Few Definitions and Limitations

Walks are easier and less exerting than *hikes*, not necessarily because they are shorter but because they involve less up and down. Several walks in this book are longer than some of the hikes. Although hike descriptions are more or less commensurate with hike lengths, walk descriptions are more idiosyncratic. They will all get you there, but some linger longer on the details of nature or culture.

Each description tells you the *length in miles* of the outing. Each hike description gives you *elapsed time*, on the grounds that you are more likely to wear a watch than a pedometer. A warning accompanies these figures, given in hours and minutes (1:37): you should add at least 20 minutes per hour, **because minutes in the book include only travel time**, not time to look at views or at historic artifacts, or for the best way to ford a brook or for an obscure blaze. Or for taking a rest. I resort to bold type because users of this book sometimes feel the pace is too fast. It is meant to be the minimum, not the optimum. The times were measured by energetic folks, unencumbered by packs, papooses, or wandering puppies.

Most of the hikes are in the woods or on mountain ridges, as are some of the walks. Of the rest, most of the walks are primarily on gravel roads. Many pass cultural sites of significance. The text hints at some cross-country skiing and road bicycling possibilities. For more on biking, pick up Lew Cuyler's *Bike Rides in the Berkshire Hills*.

This book is not a guide to the extended hiking trails in and near the county, although sections that you happen to pass over while following these routes are described. For further information, see the Appendices. The Appalachian Mountain Club and the Taconic Hiking Club publish guides to the Appalachian Trail and Taconic Crest Trail, respectively. Christopher J. Ryan has published a guide to the Taconic Trail System. See the Bibliography for these and other pertinent guides.

The trails in this book are marked by blazes. A blaze is a daub of paint or other bit of color, at about eye level usually, directly on a tree or rock—or on wood or metal attached to a tree or driven into the ground—that marks a trail. A common route for two trails may be blazed with two colors. Two blazes, one above the other, signal a sharp turn or other unusual circumstance ahead. In this county the north-south long trails are blazed white, including the Appalachian Trail; side trails to them are blazed blue; trails that don't connect to the long trails are blazed orange or red . . . with local exceptions.

The purpose of this book is to pass on information on day walks and hikes accurate as of the time I explored each of these routes, to reassure you that you are indeed on the right trail, and to encourage you—because the most important thing I learned from researching this book is that even when the weather is a bit uncertain, the distance seems a little far, you've got other things to do, or you're not feeling quite 100 percent, going out will always make you glad.

Glad because walking is good exercise for everyone. I hope this book helps you determine which distances and degrees of difficulty are healthiest for you. Glad because the scenery varies from serene to breathtaking and there is no better way to see it than to get yourself there under your own power, true personal empowerment. Most of what you will be looking at you cannot reach by car; for the rest, driving to it is no substitute for becoming a part of it. Glad because you and I need to rediscover periodically in a civilized grandeur like Berkshire where we have come from and perhaps discover some insight into where we are going.

But you already know these things.

Thanks

Special thanks to those people who provided information and to those who have been hiking and walking companions, including county residents Rebecca Barnes, Robert K. Buckwalter, Henry N. Flynt, Paul Karabinos, Allison Lassoe, Christopher Niebuhr, Bernice O'Brien, George Osgood, Robert J. Redington (who authored the section on guided trails for the blind), Robert Spencer, Edgar and Piri Taft, George S. Wislocki, Reinhard A. Wobus, and Alice Sedgwick Wohl, plus many more casual encounters and suggestions, on trail and off.

Whit Griswold's *Berkshire Trails for Walking and Ski Touring*, long out of print, introduced me to several previously unknown venues. The publishers and I thank him for making his text available as a resource. *The Berkshire Book: A Complete Guide* supplied information for several sections of this book.

Several of these hikes first appeared in an earlier version in the *Advocate* newspaper. I spent a fine morning hiking Shaker Mountain with John Manners, who rediscovered the site, researched its history, and led the Boy Scouts in laying out the trail. Deborah Burns made stylistic suggestions on early drafts of the first edition. Robert D. Hatton Jr., former county trail coordinator for the Department of Conservation and Recreation, reviewed the original material. If you spot an error, blame me—and then, please, let me know about it or other improvements in care of the publisher, so we can correct the next edition.

All the hikes and most of the walks were revisited for this, the third edition. A dozen new hikes and walks have been added.

HOW TO USE THIS BOOK

This book tries its best to be accurate and helpful. Neither the author nor the publisher can be responsible beyond that effort. Many things, both natural and man-made, are subject to change and out of the author's control. And, with the best intentions, errors are possible.

Key Terms, Important Names, Abbreviations

The word "facilities," as used here, refers to man-made structures that could be of convenience to the walker. As an example of facilities, the descriptions differentiate between flush toilets and outhouses—what the state calls pit toilets. The initials "HQ" refer to headquarters for either state-owned or privately owned properties opened to the public. The difference between "hikes" and "walks" is explained in the Introduction, as is the term "blazes," and how to read them.

CCC stands for the Civilian Conservation Corps, New Deal employment of young men that improved forests and created recreational facilities. AMC refers to the Appalachian Mountain Club, the hiking and environmentally oriented not-for-profit organization that advocates for trails and hiking in the Northeast. It is related to but not the same as the Appalachian Trail Conference, the group of local organizations that maintain the Appalachian National Scenic Trail (AT), the foot trail from Georgia to Maine. The AT passes through Berkshire County. Some of the hikes and walks in the book use parts of the footpath. While much of AT in the county runs across state land, the National Park Service has purchased stretches of land to create an AT corridor to protect the trail.

Another not-for-profit environmental organization, the Massachusetts Audubon Society, a separate entity from the

National Audubon Society, owns and maintains two sanc-
tuaries open to the public in Berkshire, both of which are
described in the text. Another major landowner is also
private, The Trustees of Reservations (TTOR), a statewide
group originally founded as analogous to a public library:
a resource available to the public for beautiful and historic
places. Five hikes or walks in this book take place on
their land.

Yet another private group, the New England Forestry
Foundation, owns the Dorothy Frances Rice Sanctuary. The
Berkshire Natural Resources Council and the Williamstown
Rural Lands Foundation both advocate for trails and own
land over which some of these walks take place. Hikes
and walks also cross the lands of Berkshire School in
Sheffield, and Buxton School and the Clark Art Institute in
Williamstown. Three hikes cross land belonging to Williams
College, in Williamstown. Walkers in the county owe a debt
to many private landowners who willingly share the enjoy-
ment of special places.

Walkers are indebted, as well, to numerous groups who
lay out, maintain and map trails, such as the Appalachian
Trail Conferences, Berkshire School, the state's Division of
Forests and Parks, the Green Mountain Club, the Williams
(College) Outing Club, and the Taconic Hiking Club of New
York—which is responsible for the Taconic Crest Trail
(TCT).

Additional Maps
To find some of the not-so-obvious corners of the
county, a supplement to regular road maps is advisable.
One is *Jimapco Map C12, Berkshire County, MA*, $4.50. It is
available in bookstores, drugstores, and newspaper stores
or from Jimapco, 2095 Route 9, Round Lake, NY 12151;
sales@jimapco.com, 1-800-MAPS 123. A lovely road map is
also available from the Registry of Deeds, Bank Row,
Pittsfield, MA 01201. (Warning: the roads are coded by own-
ership, not present condition.) Our List of Maps indicates
the U.S. Geological Survey quadrangle(s) for each hike and

walk. These maps are available directly from the survey or at bookstores and sporting goods stores. They provide the base for virtually all county maps.

Organization

Following a generally accepted tradition, this book is organized in three parts: South, Central, and North County, as shown on the maps atop each section. That should be a help in locating the hikes and walks closest to you. Here is a suggestion, however; try some farther removed. The differences you will find are interesting in their own right and helpful in defining the characteristics of your more familiar walks.

NORTH COUNTY
Adams (population 8,809)
Cheshire (3,401)
Clarksburg (1,686)
Florida (676)
New Ashford (247)
North Adams (14,681)
Savoy (705)
Williamstown (8,424)

CENTRAL COUNTY
Becket (1,755)
Dalton (6,892)
Hancock (721)
Hinsdale (1,872)
Lanesborough (5,989)
Lenox (5,077)
Peru (821)
Pittsfield (45,793)
Richmond (1,604)
Washington (541)
Windsor (875)

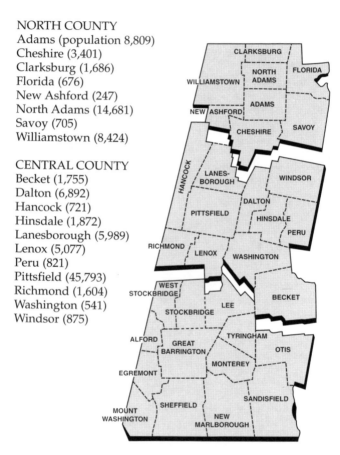

SOUTH COUNTY
Alford (399)
Egremont (1,345)
Great Barrington (7,527)
Lee (5,985)
Monterey (934)
Mount Washington (130)

New Marlborough (1,494)
Otis (1,365)
Sandisfield (824)
Sheffield (3,335)
Stockbridge (2,276)
Tyringham (350)
West Stockbridge (1,416)

BERKSHIRE ACCESS

Using Tanglewood (on the Stockbridge-Lenox line) as the
Berkshire reference point, the following cities are this close.

CITY	TIME	MILES
Albany	1 hour	50
Boston	2½ hours	135
Bridgeport	2 hours	110
Danbury	1¾ hours	85
Hartford	1½ hours	70
Montreal	5 hours	275
New Haven	2½ hours	115
New York City	3 hours	150
Philadelphia	4½ hours	230
Providence	2½ hours	125
Springfield	¾ hour	35
Waterbury	1½ hours	75
Washington, DC	7 hours	350
Worcester	1¾ hours	90

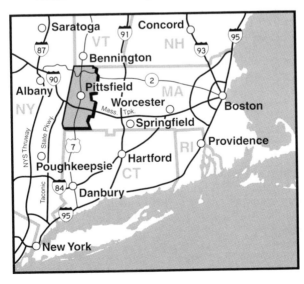

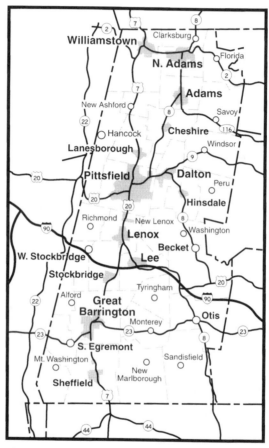

Berkshire County is 56 miles south to north, from Sheffield to Williamstown. Depending on the season and the weather, it's normally a two-hour leisurely drive up Route 7. Because of the mountain ranges that run along this route, east-west travel across the county remains much more difficult, with all the county's east-west routes (2 in the north; 9, mid-county; and 23 in the south) being tricky drives in freezing or snowy weather.

TRANSPORTATION

Getting to the Berkshires

Most people will arrive by car. *From the south:* Go north on one of the most beautiful roadways in the world, the Taconic State Parkway. For southern Berkshire, exit the Taconic at "Hillsdale, Claverack, Route 23," and follow Route 23 east, toward Hillsdale and on to Great Barrington. For Stockbridge, Lee, and Lenox proceed up Route 7. For Pittsfield and northern Berkshire, exit the Taconic at Route 295, to Route 22, following Route 22 north to Route 20 for Pittsfield or to Route 43 through Hancock to Williamstown and North Adams.

Route 7 north was an early stagecoach thoroughfare to Berkshire, and you join the same trail at Danbury, via I-684 and I-84. To arrive in southeastern Berkshire, Route 8 is a quick and scenic drive as it follows the Farmington River north.

From Boston and east: The scenic Massachusetts Turnpike (MassPike, I-90) is the quickest, easiest route west to south Berkshire and Pittsfield. Most people exit either at Lee or West Stockbridge. Farther to the north, eastern entry to Berkshire County can be gained by driving the Mohawk Trail, also known as Route 2.

A bus from Manhattan: Bonanza (1-800-556-3815) serves the Berkshires out of New York City's *Port Authority Bus Terminal* (212-564-8484) at 40th Street between 8th and 9th Avenues. Tickets may be purchased at the Greyhound ticket windows (212-971-6363), near 8th Avenue. The ride takes about 3.5 hours.

From Boston: Peter Pan/Trailways runs daily to Pittsfield and Lee-Lenox out of the Trailways Terminal at

South Station. Change to *Bonanza* in Springfield for North Adams–Williamstown. For prices and schedules contact 1-800-343-9999 or www.peterpanbus.com. Also about 3.5 hours.

Pittsfield's new intermodal center brings local and long-distance buses together with Amtrak on Columbus Avenue between North and Center Streets.

By train, commuters ride at a fraction of the regular rate if they take *Metro North* out of Grand Central Station and get off at Wassaic, New York (on Route 22 near Sharon, Connecticut). You can do the same. *Amtrak* (1-800-USA-RAIL, 413-872-7245) can also help you get to the Berkshires. Their Turboliner from Pennsylvania Station runs frequently and smoothly along the Hudson River, a splendid ride. For southern Berkshire, stay aboard till Hudson, a river town recently restored; for northern Berkshire, stay on to Rensselaer. For travel connections from Wassaic, Hudson, or Rensselaer to the Berkshires, you may require a taxi or limousine.

From Boston: Amtrak continues to run a single train daily through the Berkshires, starting from Boston's South Station, although the run is threatened.

Three aviation companies in Berkshire County operate air taxi service to just about any other northeastern airport:

Berkshire Aviation . . . . .Great Barrington Airport
413-528-1010, 528-1061
Lyon Aviation .Pittsfield Airport
413-443-6700
Shamrock Flying Service . .Harriman and West Airport
North Adams, 413-663-3330

LODGING AND DINING

Berkshire offers a host of possibilities for lodging and dining, from the humble to the luxurious. The popularity of the area as a tourist destination means that those who want to visit in the high seasons (summer and fall) must plan ahead. Lodging reservations are particularly important. We recommend two approaches to finding a place to stay and deciding where to eat. *The Berkshire Book: A Complete Guide*, from the same author and publishers of this hiking guide, is a thoroughly researched travel book, covering not only lodging and dining, but culture, recreation, shopping, and many other topics as well. The *New York Times* said its recommendations were "right on the money." It is available from bookstores throughout the United States or from the publisher. Or you can call the Berkshire Visitors Bureau (413-743-4500; 1-800-237-5747; 8 Hoosac Street, Adams, MA 01220; www.berkshires.org) to ask for their package of brochures about lodging and dining possibilities. Both *The Berkshire Book* and the Visitors Bureau provide telephone numbers for Chamber of Commerce and other lodging reservations services.

Don't forget that one of the best dining possibilities for hikers and walkers is the well-planned picnic along the trail. Berkshire offers several traditional country general stores where you can get provisions, or, if you like, elegant gourmet picnics-to-go can be ordered from many of the area's upscale grocers and caterers.

SAFETY

Walking and hiking are two of the safest and healthiest activities you might engage in. Compared to driving a car, working in the kitchen, cutting firewood . . . your chances of being injured in the slightest are extremely small. That is the way it should be: walking should be a worry-free, noncompetitive, relaxing avocation. Walking doesn't even lead to pimples.

This section ought to stop right here, without borrowing trouble. Nevertheless, after wandering around the county for several decades, I have accumulated a small amount of wisdom that could, conceivably, save you an equal amount of discomfort.

A Few Basic Rules

I want to share with you some things you probably already know but of which you may need to be reminded. I'll do it as succinctly as possible. They are all summed up in rule number one.

1. Take a few minutes before you go out to think through what you're going to do.
2. Carry water. You can't be certain even of lovely mountain brooks.
3. Wear comfortable, stout shoes or boots—not sandals, sneakers, or running shoes.
4. Remember that it may get warmer or cooler, especially on ridges.
5. Always tell someone where you are going.
6. Signs and blazes are constructions of man and cannot always be trusted. Leave the cares of civilization behind but take along a map such as the ones in this book, a compass, and a watch.

7. Stay on the trail.
8. Do not leave any trash.

These rules and this book ought to get you where you want to go . . . and back.

A special few words for newcomers to Berkshire. Welcome! Are there any dangers lurking on the roadside or in the woods? Yes, a few.

In the extreme southwestern part of the county rattlesnakes live on the rock outcroppings. This book warns you on which trails they might be encountered. *They* warn you if you are getting too near. Should you get bitten you have time to get to help from just about anywhere described here, which you should do in an unhurried but deliberate manner.

You might see a bear, which will usually run from you, especially if you make some noise (they are nearsighted). Although ours are normally mild-mannered black bears, some have been fed by humans and are therefore unpredictable. Do not try to approach a bear.

Some people are allergic to some kinds of bees. If so, they should carry a bee sting kit. In 40 years of walking in Berkshire I have never seen a rattler; bear only a few times; only once in the woods have I been stung by bees. Ticks that carry Lyme disease are rife in Berkshire County. Tuck your trousers into your socks and inspect yourself after outings. They are very small, but you can see them when they move.

Poison ivy grows in openings at lower elevations. Poison ivy leaves are illustrated here, so that you will know what to avoid.

Poison Ivy

Because of the terrain, storms can arrive without much warning—more of a potential problem in the winter than the summer. Take along extra clothes.

Hunting

Stay out of the woods and even off gravel roads during hunting season. Check at the local town hall for the dates, because Massachusetts, Connecticut, New York, and Vermont each has a different schedule and each state has a variety of seasons for different animals and weapons. In general, be on the alert from mid-November through mid-December, especially during shotgun deer season, which attracts the most two-legged participants. Sunday hunting is prohibited in Massachusetts, however.

Automobiles

Walk against traffic on roads. Wear reflective clothing at dusk. If you are parking your car, be certain the shoulder is firm. Lock your car. If you don't like to take your keys with you for fear of losing them, remember that losing your keys, while annoying, is ultimately less of a problem than losing your car.

Weather

Mark Twain, who ought to know because he summered in Tyringham, said of local weather, if you don't like it, wait five minutes. He exaggerated. Berkshire weather does grow less predictable as you gain elevation, however, and summer thunderstorms or winter snow squalls can come out of nowhere. Normally you would expect county weather to be affected by its proximity (less than 150 miles) to the ocean. Because of the hills, however, this area is controlled more by the prevailing westerly wind. Thus winters are colder and summers are cooler than either east or south of Berkshire.

Average temperature

October	49.3
January	21.2
April	44.3
July	68.3

Average precipitation
>   Snow   70″
>   Rain   36.14″
>   Total   43.14″

Clothing

It is not necessary to invest heavily in trendy clothing, although don't stop if you enjoy shopping. Consider the likelihood that the weather will change on your walk. Wear layers. If that means taking a small pack, well, that pack can also carry camera, snack, small first-aid kit, extra socks, and rain gear. A pair of well-broken-in, comfortable boots or shoes is your single most important piece of equipment. These shoes are worth some extra time, applying neat's-foot oil or waterproofing. Some hikers prefer to wear thicker socks over thin, so that friction occurs between the layers rather than between your heel and the sock.

Trail Indicators

Most trails in the county are well marked, which means that the next blaze is generally visible from the previous one. Don't keep going if you run out of blazes. Dry creek beds look deceptively like paths. While a blowdown can disrupt a path, forcing a temporary detour, thanks to the hard work of many volunteers the trails described in this book are kept in good shape. So if what you're on doesn't seem like a trail anymore, turn back until you find hard evidence that you're going the right way.

Useful Items in the Woods

In addition to water, map, compass, and watch, as noted in Basic Rules 2 and 6 above, a jackknife, matches, and small flashlight might also come in handy. As well as providing stability and a little extra push when needed, a walking stick can check the ground ahead for dampness and fend off the blows of Little John, should you run into him while crossing the Housatonic on a log. Bring a book to read while leisurely soaking up the ambiance.

First Aid

I am just as confused as you about what insect repellents really work. I prefer to stick with herbs and stay away from chemicals. What you don't wear—such as shampoo, perfume, aftershave lotion—can also be important. If you make yourself smell like a flower, you are likely to attract bugs. Your first-aid kit should include an antiseptic ointment, bandages large enough to cover a blister on your foot, and a wrap for a strain. As mentioned above, the latest word on snake bite is to get to a hospital rather than trying to treat it in the field; avoid poison ivy, bees, Lyme ticks, and bears.

After reading all this, you know as much as the natives.

BERKSHIRE HISTORY

Both natural history and social history in Berkshire are tales of ups and downs. Looking at both from the beginning of the 21st century, you may feel some past time was better than the present, but it ain't necessarily so. The county testifies that geography, for all our veneer of civilization, is still destiny. And this county, now, maintains a delicate balance of being close but not too close to the Boston–Washington megalopolis that holds down the East Coast. It is an accessible hinterland. It has the position and the resources to rise up into the future.

Six hundred million years ago the area was down, under the ocean, which was at work forming the rocks. It was warm and wet, with sandy beaches and clear, shallow waters. The lapping waves built up beaches that turned to sandstone, which in turn metamorphosed into quartzite — the erosion-resistant backbone of many of the county's ridges. Shelled marine animals built coral reefs, which calcified into limestone. The deposits of this alkaline agent, still mined on the side of Mount Greylock in Adams, protect the area from the worst ravages of acid precipitation today. Some of that limestone was recrystalized into marble, snowy chunks of which grace the hiking trails and can be inspected at the Natural Bridge in Clarksburg. Muddy offshore sediments settled to form shales and then schists, crystalline rocks that fracture cleanly. The bands of granite that run through the southern part of the county antedate the metamorphic rock.

The continents began to shift, in response to subterranean pressure. At a speed of about an inch a year over 150 million years, the land masses that would one day be North America, Africa, and Europe moved toward each other, closing the proto-Atlantic ocean. Several arcs of offshore volcanic islands were shoved onto the continent by a series of slow but cataclysmic collisions known as the Taconic Orogeny (mountain building). The entire continental shelf was squeezed into a series of folds, the monumental fore-runners of the Appalachian Range. The bases of these mountains, some Himalayan in height, must have just about filled Berkshire, when the county reached for the sky. Then the continents began to pull apart, as they are still doing.

As soon as mountains were stacked up, the process of erosion began. Rain fell, forming rivers that still drain these hills, but in those days more vigorously carving a landscape unrooted by vegetation. Not only water but wind sculpted Berkshire hills, raging unbroken by trees and shrubs. The rugged landscape was tamed, waiting only for plants to soften it.

Less than two million years ago the first of a succession of four ice sheets ground down in response to a cooling climate. These mile-high glaciers brought debris, gravel and rocks, which they deposited around the nubbins of mountains that remained. Glacial lakes covered most of North County and a good portion of the south. Because the Hoosac Valley was pre-glacial, once the melt set in, the Hoosic River returned to flowing across the path of the ice. It therefore stands an an anomaly in New England, where most of the rivers run north to south as a result of the glacial combing. Nor were the beds of the Housatonic or Westfield much altered. The Farmington River ran up against a load of glacial trash that turned its general southerly course in Connecticut.

The ice withdrew as recently as 10,000 years ago. Vegetation and then wildlife followed its retreating edge. Perhaps a few of the earliest North American inhabitants, having boated or walked across the land bridge from Asia, were in Berkshire to bid farewell to the ice. Gradually, the evergreen forest moved north, lingering only on the tops of the highest ridges, while the broad-leaved, deciduous forest moved in, characterized in North County by sugar maple and in the south by oak, with their associated pines, ash, beech, birch and alder.

The rocky steepness of the county does not lend itself to leisurely flowing water and big lakes. With the exception of the southern reach of the Housatonic, which meanders in through Sheffield, Berkshire rivers retain little water and rush to their destinations. What lakes the county has, it owes to the efforts of 19th-century industrialists to create a head or a reservoir to provide a year-round flow of water for power or other manufacturing processes: Otis Reservoir, Cheshire Reservoir, Pontoosuc, Onota, and others.

Seen from above, the county presents the ridges that remain from the north-south running folds: the Taconics along the New York line, the lower end of the Green Mountains protruding over the Vermont line, the Hoosacs filling the northeast quadrant, the Southern Berkshire Plateau filling the southeast quadrant, and a line of river valleys, just to the left of center, made up of the Hoosic and Housatonic—albeit flowing in opposite directions—that meet in New Ashford.

The Greylock massif stands as a peninsula to the Taconics—as indeed it was when glacial Lake Bascom filled the Hoosac Valley up to the 1,300-foot contour. Therefore it may be appropriate that the summit of Greylock lifts a War Memorial Tower, its design influenced by lighthouses, bearing a beacon that can be seen by people navigating most of the county. If any man-made feature is needed to unite a geographical area so well defined topographically, it would be that tower and the roads it guards (Routes 2, 7, and 8).

Getting in and out of and around Berkshire used to be a problem. The native Americans generally thought of the area as removed from their Hudson River homes, a hunting ground to visit in the summer. The Mahicans entered from the south or north, along the river valleys. Although the Bay Colony claimed the land early on, Bay Colony residents found it tough to surmount the Berkshire barrier to the east. Early European settlers found it easier to enter along the valleys, a few Dutch infiltrating through the Taconics from New

York, but especially residents from the area now known as Connecticut, up the Housatonic. Thus the county was settled from the south to the north, the earliest towns in the south dating to the first quarter of the 18th century. The main roads, railroads, and even sewer lines now follow the valleys.

The Europeans were primarily farmers, typically work-ing the bottom lands and, as they filled up, moving up the sides of the hills. Remains of walls, cellar holes, and orchards such as you come across in your ambles remind you that even what now seem lofty ridges were at one time home, especially for those who made their living grazing cattle or merino sheep. In Stockbridge, the English Society for the Propagation of the Gospel in Foreign Parts set up an Indian mission, which gradually acceded to the land hunger of the Europeans. By the time of the Revolution, virtually all native Americans had departed.

As a farmer installed a mill to grind his corn or saw his wood, and his neighbors came to have him do their milling, so industry followed the plow. What began as groupings to protect against French or Indian raids became trading cen-ters. Specialty manufactures based on natural resources developed, such as glass, paper, charcoal, and textiles. Even education can be seen as a Berkshire industry depending on natural resources. After all, Thoreau said of Williams College's position at the foot of Greylock: "It would be no small advantage if every college were thus located at the base of a mountain, as good at least as one well-endowed professorship. . . . Some will remember, no doubt, not only that they went to college, but that they went to the moun-tain." In Berkshire County, the four colleges and many of the secondary schools are at the base of mountains.

The opening of the Erie Canal in 1825, providing a prac-tical means for younger residents to head west where the thick topsoil had a lot fewer glacial stones than that of Berkshire, drained the county of human resources. One by one lamps winked out on the sidehill farms. Whereas by the middle of the 19th century three-quarters of the trees had been stripped for pasture land or to feed the insatiable

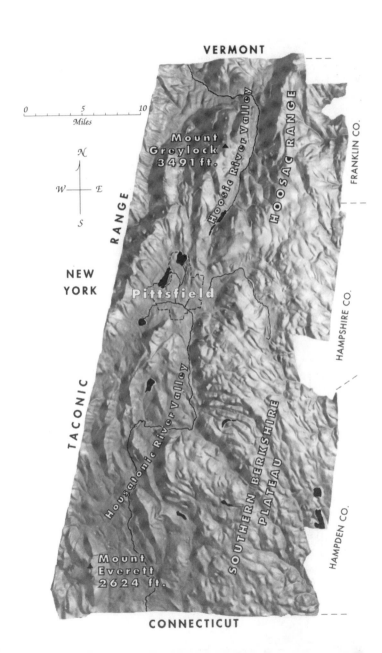

maws of the railroad, the county has been revegetating for 150 years. In Berkshire that ratio is inverted today. The county is three-quarters wooded, which is why coyote, bear, beaver, turkey, and even moose are returning to join the populous deer and smaller animals.

The most important industrial event in the county's history happened in 1886, when William Stanley linked 25 shops along the main street of Great Barrington in the world's first commercial electric system. That, in turn, drew the General Electric Company to Stanley's shop in Pittsfield. GE has been here ever since, although much reduced today. The second most important industrial event was the opening of the Hoosac Tunnel, at 4.75 miles the longest bore in the world in 1875, breaking through the Berkshire barrier for direct train service in the North County between Boston and Albany.

Yet even in the heady days when industry was king—the population of Pittsfield growing from 25,000 to 58,000 in the first 60 years of the 20th century—second homes, tourism, and culture were already crowned princes. In the Gilded Age that ended the 19th century, wealthy families collected great estates and built luxury palaces, known as "cottages," some 75 in Lenox and Stockbridge. Major literary figures toured the county: Emerson, Melville, Hawthorne, Holmes, Thoreau, Wharton, Twain—some settled here. Actors, musicians, and artists followed, and are still following.

As the county now, somewhat painfully, recognizes that industries will never again be what they were through World War II, it is coming to rely on a service economy to which, at least, it is no stranger. Filled with fine educational institutions, public and private, with museums and musicians, with art and artifacts to grace the green walls installed infinitely earlier by nature, Berkshire's streams are cleaner and woods thicker than since farms and industry first came to these garrison hills. And the hills retain a plentiful supply of ground water, likely to become increasingly important to the future of this area.

Berkshire has now, as it has had since the ice left, an indigenous population that cares deeply for the land—witness the many towns in the county that have long had zoning, have now established land trusts, and are considering land use countywide. Berkshire residents listen attentively at town meetings to discussions of protecting ridges and aquifers, saving farmland, and cleaning up hazardous waste. Little litter mars the many paths. Whether driving its roads or walking its trails, you will soon get the message that this land is cared for.

SOUTH COUNTY

SOUTH COUNTY

MOUNT WASHINGTON

Mount Washington, the smallest town by population in the Commonwealth of Massachusetts, has 130 residents. It contains 6,500 acres of state land—like the towns of Washington, Savoy, and New Ashford, about half the town is state owned. Perched at a 2,000-foot elevation, like Savoy and Windsor, it is a town formed by its topography. The town may have been settled first by Dutch moving east from the Hudson River as early as 1692. That would make it the oldest town in Berkshire, but the point is disputed. In any case, the mountain men who lived there about 1730 preferred to consider themselves Bay Colony residents, where individuals owned their land, rather than subject to the feudal tenure of the Hudson Valley. Hudson lord Robert Livingston sent a party onto the mountain in 1755 to extract rents deeded him by the governor of New Amsterdam. A skirmish broke out. Pioneer William Race, for whom Mount Race and Race Brook were probably named, was killed. In 1761 Livingston's men burned six homes in Mount Washington. In spite of the fact that the town was incorporated in 1781, the dispute continued until the New York–Massachusetts boundary was settled in 1787.

In the 1840s and '50s inhabitants earned their living by cutting trees and making charcoal; later, they farmed potatoes; now they drive down off their mountain to work at jobs elsewhere. The scenery is spectacular—a phrase not often used even in a book limited to the best of Berkshire. What a place to begin!

Camping

Part of the charm of Mount Washington is the absence of any tourist facilities. There is a state-owned cabin on the trail between the two peaks of Alander that can be used on a first-come, first-served basis. The primitive camping area on the Alander Trail is lovely for tenting (no facilities). Camping is available at the New York end of the two-state Bash Bish Park, with facilities. A cabin is available to AMC members (reserved in advance) off East Road near Sage's Ravine. There are campsites along the AT at Sage's Ravine, Laurel Ridge, and Race Brook; a shelter is available just north of Mount Everett at Glen Brook.

HIKES

ALANDER MOUNTAIN/BASH BISH FALLS

7 miles (3 hours hiking time), plus 4.5 miles to complete loop

Road approaches

Take Route 41 south from South Egremont village, but turn right just past the pond, on Mount Washington Road. (There is a state forest sign.) After 3 miles, the road swings southerly and begins to climb to a ridge. Signs help at the intersections, but essentially head straight to the Mount Washington State Forest HQ, on the right 9 miles from the village. Park there. If you choose to make this a two-car expedition, which is recommended, take the signed road right at the church (before forest HQ) to Bash Bish Falls upper (first paved) parking lot (7.5 miles). Leave car No. 1 there; drive No. 2 back to forest HQ.

ALANDER MOUNTAIN

The extremes of this hike, Alander Mountain and Bash Bish Falls, are remarkable by any set of criteria. The open

Bash Bish Falls, Alander Hike

ridge of the mountain (2,239 feet) has a fine view west to the Catskills and, if the weather is clear, even to the tall buildings in Albany, New York, 50 miles northwest. As you hike north from the summit, continual twists in the trail reveal new views, especially the intimate one down into Valley View Farm. The waters of Bash Bish Brook plunge 200 feet at the falls, the most spectacular in Berkshire, divided partway down by a pulpit-like granite outcropping before tumbling into a pool and thence to other riffles and pools downstream. (The falls are always worth seeing, although the amount of water varies considerably: most in spring and fall.)

The Alander Trail is well worn from the Mount Washington State Forest HQ parking lot, where you can also register to use the campground. Follow west the triangular blue blazes the state uses to mark hiking trails, across a field, into a woods, and out into another field. At this point you are on what is virtually a road. At nine minutes, cross a brook on a bridge and continue on the road, passing the Ashley Hill Trail, also a woods road, on your left (1 mile).

At 18 minutes you must ford a brook (you want to wear boots rather than sneakers for all hikes). Two brooks join here, with a mill foundation right. The somewhat wet trail rises moderately through hemlock forest, which gradually becomes a laurel grove, with a few birches and oaks. Old stone walls speak of a time of farms. You pass the camping area to the left at 42 minutes. This oak/laurel forest is distinctly different from the northern hardwood forest you see farther upcounty, characterized by a higher percentage of sugar maples. Similar spring ephemeral flowers are visible before the leaves come on the trees, however: the mottled leaves of trout lily; hepatica with its blue-pink-white blossoms and oddly shaped leaves; spring beauty, which has rose pink flowers with grasslike leaves; distinctive dutchman's breeches, with parsleylike leaves.

The woods road ends at a circle that marks as far as the warden could drive to get to the fire tower that once stood on Alander. You pass straight through, bearing left at a junction (both branches have blue blazes). Shortly you come to an ominous sign that says, "Last water during dry season," as the branch of the brook you are following begins to peter out. You are climbing more steeply through laurel now.

At 1:13 comes the state cabin in the notch between the south and north peaks of Alander. Just beyond is a bewildering nest of signs. Turn right, scrambling up the rocks to the western summit (3 miles from the road). Note the white blazes turning sharply north (right) but take the time to explore the area of the old fire tower footings for the different views. The major highway on which you can see traffic is Route 22 in New York State. Follow along the ridge line, north, with occasional opportunities to look east as well as west, between pitch pine and thick laurel. At 1:47 you take the first of several sharp descents, following white blazes mostly painted on the rocks. Hawks sail on the warm updrafts of this ridge. The deep gorge of Bash Bish is taking shape to the right; at some point you will start to hear the roar of the falls.

After you scramble down a steep incline (2:22), a junction gives a choice of routes to the falls. The route to the right is shorter but involves fording Bash Bish Brook and should be used only at low water (when it hasn't rained for a while). The left fork leads past an attractive overlook (still featuring Valley View Farm) and down a series of hairpin turns, through large hemlocks, into the camping area (2:49) by the shower building. Follow the white dots left, down the road to the bridge.

Massachusetts purchased the 400 acres around the falls in 1924; then, during the 1960s, 4,000 more acres to make up Mount Washington State Forest. Since New York State owns land just downstream in Copake Falls (and manages the camping area), this was the first example of these two states jointly maintaining a park (a second exists at Petersburgh Pass, west of Williamstown).

Follow the gravel road upstream from the parking lot to the falls (3:09). Stone steps lead down to the most dramatic view. Be warned: the guardrails are intended to keep you on

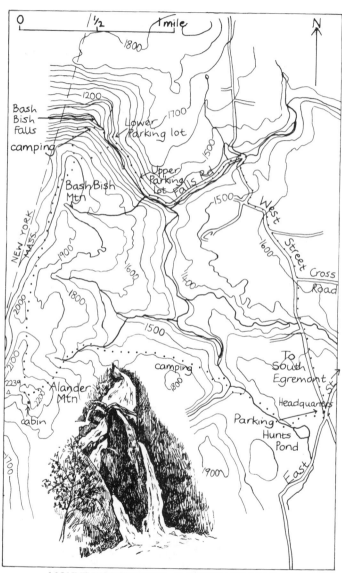

MOUNT WASHINGTON: ALANDER MOUNTAIN/
BASH BISH FALLS

the trails. Several people trying to climb the cliffs or dive into the pools have killed themselves. Rock climbing is allowed only with permission of the park ranger. In addition, rattlesnakes have been found in the vicinity.

Ten more minutes take you upstream to the upper parking lot, a good place to explore the lookouts. The gorge is colonnaded with large hemlocks, some of them clinging to what appears to be nothing but rock. Like every good county cliff, Bash Bish has a myth of an Indian maiden. In this case, Bash Bish was accused of adultery and strapped into a canoe at the head of the falls as punishment. Just as the canoe was about to go over, the sun formed a halo about her head and butterflies gathered. Indians found the remains of the canoe in the pool at the bottom but not her body. The falls still say her name, if you listen closely.

This Taconic ridge on the state's border is part of the Appalachians, pushed up when the continents collided and worn down by erosion ever since. Bash Bish Brook was formed by the melting of the last glacier, 10,000 to 12,000 years ago. The quartz dike, halfway up the falls, was forced out of the earth 400 million years ago. As the sediment in the brook works in the water, it gradually destroys Bash Bish Falls.

You probably would just as soon get into No. 1 car here, as the walk by road to forest HQ is 4.5 more miles, up Falls Road and right on West Street. A short cut, shown on old maps, along Bash Bish Brook to the Alander Trail (3 miles back to HQ), unfortunately crosses posted property belonging to the Mount Washington Club. It is not blazed, signed, or completely maintained. As an alternative to two cars, you could leave a bicycle at Bash Bish (but the climb would be steep).

MOUNT EVERETT

5.5 miles (4.75 hours hiking time), plus 2 miles to complete loop

Road approaches

Although most of the hike is in the uplands of the town of Mount Washington, it begins at the Berkshire School, just off Route 41 in Sheffield. The hike ends at a parking area about 2 miles down the road, where the Race Brook Falls Trail comes out. So you could use two cars or you could walk between the beginning and end or, best idea, you could bring a bike, dropping the car at the Race Brook trail-head. The bike ride to the school on a fairly level road through lovely farm fields, looking up at the steep sides of the mountain, is pleasant.

To get to Berkshire School, take Berkshire School Road, appropriately enough, out of Sheffield and jog north on Route 41 or, from the north, take Routes 23 and 41 west from Great Barrington. Bear south where 23 continues west, just after South Egremont. The school is 3.5 miles south of the junction.

MOUNT EVERETT

Mount Everett (2,602 feet) is the outstanding peak in Berkshire County south of the Greylock massif. Although the fire tower has been removed, views extend in most directions from the generally open summit, as well as from the Appalachian Trail (AT) to the north and especially the south. The slopes are steep on this 5.5-mile hike, so you want to wear good footgear, especially for climbing over the rock outcroppings.

As an alternative, a gravel automobile road climbs very near the summit from East Street in Mount Washington. Call 413-528-0330 to find out if the road is open. You could drive into the reservation to picnic at

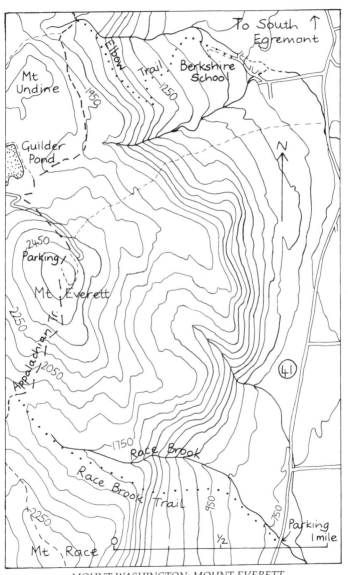

MOUNT WASHINGTON: MOUNT EVERETT

Guilder Pond and walk to the summit from the pond or from the end of the road. It would also be possible to walk north on the AT, to be met at Berkshire School, or south on the AT to be met at the Race Brook trailhead, having let the car do most of the climbing.

Berkshire School (850 feet in elevation) is most attractive, set into the side of the hills and fronted by rolling, mowed lawns. An education there comes complete with ski and hiking trails. The students maintain the Elbow Trail. You should stay on the trails, because rattlesnakes have been seen in the area.

To get to visitor parking at the school, bear right at the admissions building, past the tennis court and behind the hockey rink. You may have to ask directions to the trailhead, but you want to walk back toward admissions. Before you get that far, follow the service road by the north end of the main building. Go past a home and straight at a hard left in the gravel road. The Elbow Trail is blazed blue, about five minutes from parking.

The trail runs 1.2 miles to the AT, through hemlock woods, gradually increasing in steepness. At the elbow (15 minutes from the house), take a hard right on the blue-blazed trail, which meets the AT .5 mile farther north (35 minutes from the parking lot). Turn left (south) on the AT, blazed white. From the Elbow Trail to the summit it's 1.8 miles. In 30 minutes from arriving on the AT you will reach the road up Mount Everett at the Guilder Pond picnic area/parking lot (including an outhouse).

Most of the rest of the way to the summit the trail parallels the road, until the road stops and those who drive join you on foot for the last quarter mile. Note that the AT turns left at an old tower site (1:25 minutes). You may want to explore, right, to the site of a tower taken down in 2003. Over the low shrubbery, including blueberry, scrub oak, and pitch pine, you catch fine views of Alander Mountain to the west, Mount Frissel to the south, and, if you move around, other views as well. On a clear day, the Catskills are visible across the Hudson River. The foundations for the old tower make a picnic site with vistas.

The descent south from the summit provides the most exciting views of the Berkshire and Litchfield Hills, and of the Housatonic River as it snakes into Connecticut. The going is moderately difficult, dropping down steeply over schist with marble outcroppings. The blue-blazed trail, left, where the brook crosses, .7 mile from the summit (30 minutes), takes you through a camping area and down Race Brook Trail to Route 41.

You cross a two-log bridge, under large hemlocks, after 15 minutes on Race Brook Trail, as the brook takes form in the wetlands. This interesting process gives you a graphic idea of the meaning of "watershed." At the top of the falls the trail turns left, but you may want to explore this scenic spot. The trail climbs to a lookout (55 minutes) with a view into Sheffield. You cross below the upper falls—five falls (cascades, really) all together descend perhaps 1,300 feet into the valley.

The trail (marked with blue blazes) works its way down the side of the ravine from the upper falls, through the laurel and large hemlocks, coming out at the paved parking area, for a total hiking time of 2.75 hours (not counting pausing for the views). Partway down, a loop trail leads to the lower falls.

Turn left on Route 41. There is ample shoulder to walk on. The school, remember, is on the left, a bit beyond where Berkshire School Road enters right.

SHEFFIELD

The southernmost town center in the county is also generally accepted as the oldest (1726); it's no coincidence when you consider that most of the earliest settlers to Berkshire came from Connecticut. In 1725, Matthew Noble arrived alone from Westfield to make friends with the American Indians, clear the land, and erect a cabin. Next he fetched his daughter and returned on horseback to set up the first home in Berkshire (then still part of Hampshire County). The first struggles were with the New York Dutch, who regarded western Berkshire as their own. In 1735, settlers raised the meeting house on Sheffield Plain, a mile north of the present village center.

Sheffield earned the distinction of being the first County Seat or Shire town when Berkshire became its own county in 1761 and watched that distinction move gradually north, from Great Barrington to Lenox to Pittsfield. Sheffield had its bout with industry, as is true of most Berkshire towns. Marble from quarries in Ashley Falls adorns the customhouse in Boston and the courthouse in New York City. Daniel Shays's Rebellion, a movement of Revolutionary War veterans who felt they had been insufficiently compensated for their services, failed in battle with government troops in Sheffield in 1789.

The town exported its sons. Chester Dewey trained for four years at Williams College in the fields (literally) in which he was famous in the first half of the 19th century: botany and geology. Another son, Frederick Augustus Porter Barnard, president of Columbia University, determined that Columbia should include women. Barnard College was named for him shortly after he died in 1889.

Camping

Numerous tenting sites exist in conjunction with the Appalachian Trail in this vicinity: those just south of the summit of Bear Mountain, at Sage's Ravine, and Laurel

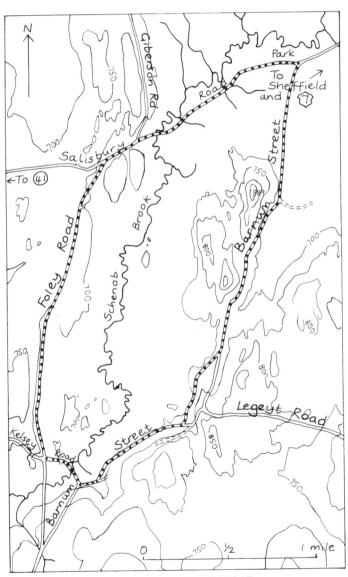

SHEFFIELD: SALISBURY ROAD

Ridge are on the route described for hiking Bear Mountain. The Bond shelter is nearby to the south and the Glen Brook shelter is north, over the summit of Mount Everett.

WALKS

SALISBURY ROAD

7 miles (2.5 hours)

A most attractive stroll of a serious dimension but generally level, with mixed wooded and open landscape, begins at the junction of Salisbury and Barnum Roads. It would make a fine bicycle route. Take Berkshire School Road or Root Lane west from the center of town. Both shortly run into Salisbury Road, which you should follow left. Park where Barnum, soon to become gravel, enters. Walk along Salisbury to Foley Road, which bears left. Follow that gravel road to a tangle of roads that cross Schenob Brook. You will pass some lovely real farms and a few gentrified farms, all with distinguished vistas, particularly of Mount Everett. To make your way through the maze, just keep turning left. You will end up on Barnum Street and, in another 2 miles, at your automobile.

BARTHOLOMEW'S COBBLE AND COLONEL JOHN ASHLEY HOUSE

Various trails available

These two adjacent properties of The Trustees of Reservations are south of the Sheffield town center, near the village of Ashley Falls on the Connecticut line. Turn right on Route 7A, then shortly veer right over railroad tracks onto Rannappo Road; continue straight to Cooper Hill Road and turn right. The Col. John Ashley House is the oldest still-existing dwelling in Berkshire County, built in 1735. Col. Ashley led troops at the Battle of Bennington (1777).

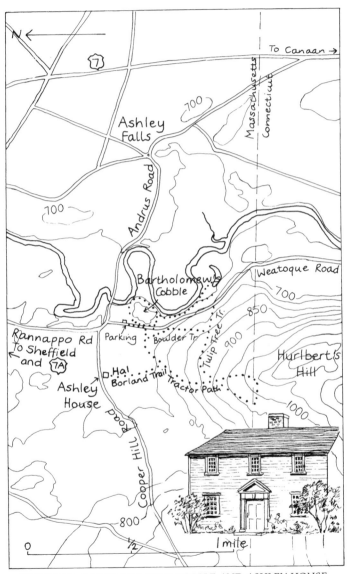

SHEFFIELD: BARTHOLOMEW'S COBBLE AND ASHLEY HOUSE

The Sheffield Declaration, written at the Ashley House, preceded the Declaration of Independence by three years. Theodore Sedgwick, originally of Sheffield but later of Stockbridge, successfully defended two of the Ashley slaves, Mum Bett and Brom, who sought freedom under a "born free and equal" clause in the state's constitution. That decision led to the freedom of other slaves in the state. The house is open seasonally for guided tours. Note the remarkable collection of tools in the attic.

The Borland Trail joins the Ashley property with the Bartholomew's Cobble trails. These otherwise can be reached by continuing straight at Cooper Hill Road to Weatogue Road, just a matter of a few hundred yards, to a parking area on the left. A large map of the Trustees' property shows numerous trails. The ones around the Cobble itself, the rocky eminence between the parking lot and the Housatonic River, are shorter and steeper. These show a remarkable variety of wild flowers and shrubs growing in the rich river bottomland, which is laced with limestone. Bartholomew's Cobble is considered one of the nation's outstanding concentrations of native plants: more than 700 species, including 44 ferns and fern allies. Bird-watchers have spotted more than 250 species here.

Trails also range across Weatogue Road on open fields and through wooded land. The fields are home to deer and cows, which are sometimes curious but not dangerous. The fences have British-type stiles that enable you to pass where cattle can't. It is possible to stroll about 2 miles, generally following white blazes, up the tractor path to the summit of Hurlbert's Hill, from which there is a lovely view centered on Mount Everett; then return by the Tulip Tree Trail, which crosses Weatogue Road and returns you to the maze of trails by the river. You can cover many of the trails in two hours, allowing time to pause for the flora. Try to visit the Cobble in the spring, when the many ephemeral flowers—those that come out before the leaves on the trees shade them—are blossoming, but before the summer traffic hits.

TTOR charges a small fee for a tour of the Ashley house and even less to tramp the Cobble.

HIKE

BEAR MOUNTAIN

Sheffield and Salisbury, Connecticut, 10 miles (4.75 hours hiking time)

Road approaches

Best as a two-car trip. Park the first at the Race Brook Falls trailhead, 2 miles south of Berkshire School on Route 41 (see Mount Everett). Drive the second car about 7.5 miles south, or 1.5 miles beyond the Connecticut border. Look sharp on the right for an opening into a parking area marked by a small, blue sign that reads "Undermountain Trail." There is a kiosk and a privy.

BEAR MOUNTAIN

Hike from Connecticut into Massachusetts so that you experience first the fine views from the grand and clear summit of Bear Mountain and then those truly extraordinary views from the .5-mile ridge leading to the summit of Race Mountain. The extent of the panorama is unique in Berkshire County: the Housatonic Valley, in the two states, lies before you. (This approach means going down the steeper side of Bear and Race Mountains, however, if that is a factor.) Several lovely cascades and a gorgeous sight and smell of laurel (in season) also greet you. The access trails are each about 2 miles, connected by 6 miles of the Appalachian National Scenic Trail (AT).

The Undermountain Trail, blazed blue, ascends in a determined but moderate angle from the trailhead, wide and well traveled (the most heavily used AT access trail in Connecticut). The oak forest is open. Although you cross streams, the route is predominantly dry. In .5 hour the Paradise Lane Trail exits right. (It continues to the AT, avoiding Bear Mountain, making a summit loop possible.)

You pass over some bog bridges and through quantities of laurel, spectacularly in bloom in late May. Turn north on the AT (blazed white) at 45 minutes. The campsite trail turns right six minutes later. The view opens up and you reach the summit of Bear, 2,351 feet, in 1.75 hours. A plaque honors a stonemason whose labors yielded the monument that signifies the highest peak in Connecticut. (Mount Frissel is higher, but its summit is in Massachusetts.) Twin Lakes lie before you, as well as the curlicues of Schenob Brook, while the Housatonic River itself is obscured behind a low ridge.

The descent on the north is a steep scramble over rocks. In 20 minutes you reach Sage's Ravine and the north end of Paradise Lane. You descend to the brook through a hemlock forest. In 5 miles a bridge leads to the campsite, but you follow along the south side, a trail precarious above the brook, for about 20 minutes. Then cross the brook on stones, beginning a slow climb, partly on a woods road, with rock outcrops left. From the start, 2.5 hours takes you to the newly constructed Laurel Ridge Campsites and privy, substituting for the closed Bear Rock Falls Campsites, which were dangerously close to a precipice.

In .5 hour the view, especially on the east side, opens again as you begin the slow approach to Race Mountain. The view extends from Mount Greylock in the north to the Connecticut ridges. It is not so much a distance view, however, as it is a comprehensive look at what the Nature Conservancy calls one of the Last Great Places, a natural area of wetlands, water bodies, farmed fields, and wooded ridges. And 20 minutes later you arrive at the actual summit, 2,365 feet, nestled in pitch pine that has been dwarfed by the wind and ice.

More laurel, more oak, more hemlock, more rock brings you in 40 minutes (about 3.75 hours from the start) to the Race Brook Falls Trail, on which you turn right. Follow the brook, just forming, for 10 minutes until crossing the two-log bridge and beginning a short climb. Then down and across stones below the upper cascades (23 minutes). These are stunning and easier to view than the Lower Falls, to

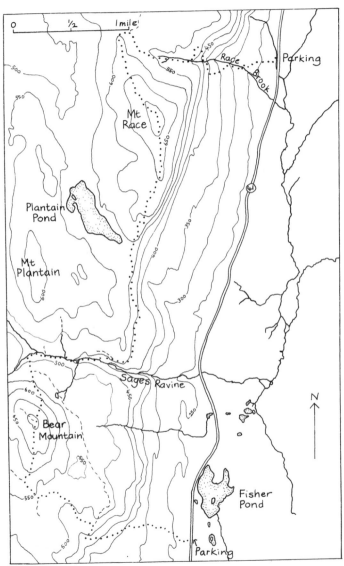

SHEFFIELD AND SALISBURY, CT: BEAR MOUNTAIN

which a loop trail leads in 12 minutes. Your trail follows close but above the brook valley, crosses the brook, and drops you in a field adjacent to the trailhead parking, 40 minutes from the "Upper Falls"—really a cascade—and 4.75 hours from the start.

EGREMONT

A township that is two villages (North and South Egremont), the Egremonts are gently rolling, even flat, compared to upland neighboring Mount Washington. But the walking is great here, offering extraordinarily long views for those who have neither the time nor the inclination to scale a peak. Back in the early history of Egremont, one man who wanted to remain on the plain was General Henry Knox, who entered Berkshire through the Egremonts in 1776, with soldiers, 124 yoke of oxen, and 58 captured cannon from Fort Ticonderoga and Crown Point—all en route to Boston to help George Washington drive out the British. These days you'll find a few good shops (including a sporting goods store, open fall and winter only) and three noteworthy restaurants in South Egremont, and one fine restaurant and a classic country general store in North Egremont.

WALKS

BALDWIN HILL ROAD NORTH AND SOUTH

6 miles or less (2.5 hours, round trip)

Start from either South or North Egremont, or station a car in each village. If you begin this round trip at the general store in North Egremont, at the corner of Route 71 and the North Egremont–Hillsdale Road (at the sign for Prospect Lake), go west through a residential area for .1 mile and turn left onto Baldwin Hill Road North and South (gravel), which rises gently for .6 mile while passing by

French Park on the right and through woods. The road flattens out as you begin to leave the woods; vistas appear in all directions. Pass pungent Bel Air Farm on the right and admire the vast cornfields. At 1.1 miles (25 minutes), cross the intersection of Baldwin Hill Road East and West. Your view includes, to the west, Catamount Ski Area; to the southwest, Mount Everett; to the south, the Litchfield Hills in Connecticut; to the east, Monument Mountain and Warner Mountain (the latter to the east of Great Barrington, which is hidden from view, down in a valley).

The road slopes gently downwards now toward South Egremont. Note the airplanes rising and descending near the Great Barrington Airport in the valley to the east. At 2 miles (50 minutes), cross the intersection with Town House Hill Road. At 2.2 miles, pass a small (private) pond left. The road is now paved and rising slightly. By 2.6 miles it's all downhill into South Egremont, where at Route 23 (3 miles, 1:15 minutes) you turn left and go 100 yards to the deli or restaurant for a snack before heading back.

Alternatives include side trips on Baldwin Hill Road East and West. Either way is good, although neither has any particular destination. Going east, you'll probably want to descend to just past a large white farmhouse in the pines right, then turn around and retrace your steps. Total mileage without the side trip is 6 (2.5 hours); with the side trip, 6.8.

JUG END

3 mile walk on loop trail (1:15 minutes)

A lovely walk, mixing open fields and deep woods, while exploring the remains of Jug End Resort. The name derives from the German word "jugend" or "youth," perhaps a multilingual pun designed to rally young people to the resort. An older name for the area is Guilder Hollow. A part of a large assemblage of open land in the Massachusetts–Connecticut–New York corner, The Nature

Conservancy locates Jug End in one of the "Last Great Places."

In South Egremont, turn south off Route 23 onto Route 41, almost immediately turning west onto Mount Washington Road. In about 1 mile turn south on Jug End Road, marked by the chocolate-colored state sign. Pass the buildings about .5 mile on right to the large parking lot. A number of trails cross this property. In case of confusion, note that you are heading up on one side of Fenton Brook and back on the other. Before the property was acquired by the state, it was a resort and ski area, explaining the trails on the far hill.

Depart the east corner of the parking lot at an old foundation and the Nature Conservancy sign; turn right on an old road, following blue blazes with black acorns. Cross a field, heading up into the woods, and another field, bearing right, looking across at Mount Danby. At 17 minutes turn left into hemlock woods off the road and in 40 minutes cross Fenton Brook at an old cabin site. Follow the jeep road downstream, beside the brook. In about one hour, come into an open field again, bear right; and again right at a small bridge. This should return you to the footbridge that leads to the parking lot.

NEW MARLBOROUGH

Benjamin Wheeler came from Marlborough, Massachusetts, in 1736, because his home town had been granted this western territory. He would have starved the first winter if some folks from Sheffield hadn't heard of his plight and struggled through the snow to his relief. But he had sufficient spirit to stick it out and invite the rest of his family to join him the next summer.

The town now has a population of 1,494, pretty well spread out. The town center is on Route 57, which drops south from Route 23 east of Great Barrington. Other village centers in New Marlborough township are Hartsville, near beautiful Lake Buel; Mill River and Konkapot on the Konkapot River; Southfield, at the junction of New Marlborough and East Hill Roads; and Gomorrah and Clayton in the south. The town has more defined villages than any other in the county. The road signs are so thorough and numerous they virtually require you to stop the car to read them, which may be just what the citizens of New Marlborough want.

WALKS

HARMON ROAD

New Marlborough and Monterey, 7 miles (2.75 hours)

A stroll begins at New Marlborough village and follows the New Marlborough–Monterey Road (bear right at the fork) into Monterey, past the Trout Pond on Harmon Brook. You are still on the road when you turn left. Turn left again on Harmon Road, back to the point of origin. This is a fine bike route. Rawson Brook Farm at the Monterey end sells goat cheese. The Old Inn on the Green, at the Marlborough end, is a lovely spot for a cool drink.

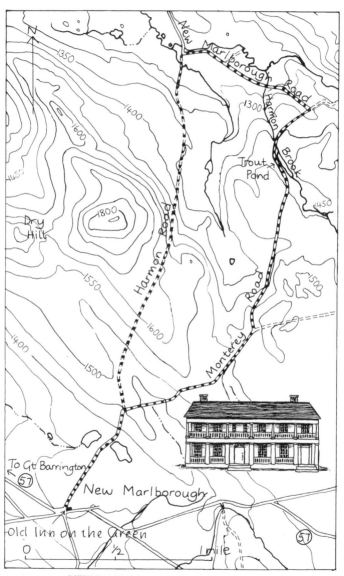

NEW MARLBOROUGH: HARMON ROAD

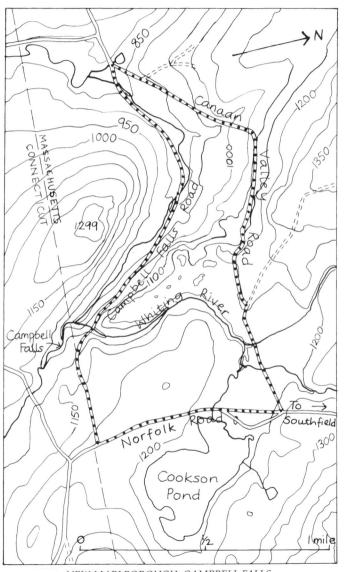

NEW MARLBOROUGH: CAMPBELL FALLS

CAMPBELL FALLS

Southfield, 4.5 miles (2 hours), although the falls are only 200 yards from parking

This walk runs through the Campbell Falls State Forest area just on the state line. Follow the Southfield Road south from New Marlborough center into the village of Southfield, and the Norfolk Road south from Southfield. Provisions and friendly information are available at the Southfield General Store. Park near Cookson Pond. Walk north on Norfolk to left on Canaan Valley Road, left on Canaan Road (both gravel), and left again on Campbell Falls Road across a bridge over Whiting Brook. A parking area marks the short side trip to the falls (which fall in Connecticut). These are worth seeing, especially at times of heavy flow. A final, brief left on Norfolk Road should complete the tour. The road through the state forest may be a bit rough, but biking is possible in season and skiing in the winter.

YORK POND

2 miles (1 hour)

South of New Marlborough, the South Sandisfield Road passes the Sandisfield State Forest. Don't go by. Stop in at one of the best public swimming areas in the county, well maintained, with clean changing rooms. (This popular area is closed when 300 swimmers assemble, so you may be turned away on a summer weekend.) Gasoline engines aren't allowed on the lake, so it is clean and inviting once it warms up. The Pond Loop Trail, which can be wet, departs from the picnic area and follows the pond to a gravel road, then doubles back on the other (and more scenic) shore. Half-mile walks from HQ lead to a former CCC camp and follow a gravel road to the grave of Josh Smith, a local resident. Other lovely walks are available on gravel roads. Just down the road is a memorial to five CCC wardens. There is a modest day-use fee or show a season pass (good at all state properties).

MONTEREY

Including as it does major lakes Buel and Garfield, both open to the public, and a good bit of Beartown State Forest, Monterey, with a year-round population of 934, has great appeal to the second-home owner. Lake Garfield was named for the U.S. president who used to summer there. Summering has increased; it's likely that on a weekend the population doubles, not that there are many hotels or motels. The center of town is pretty much defined by the general store, on Route 23. Once the center was farther north, near the home of the first minister, Adonijah Bidwell.

Among the early settlers was Isaac Benedict, who opened a tavern. Descendent Fred Benedict's ice pond was enlarged to 35 acres to be a attraction at the state forest, where it provides for swimming and small boating. Whereas in early days the Konkapot River powered wood industries, now there are no discernible industries and few businesses, except of course Rawson Brook Farm, manufacturer of goat's milk cheese, and Gould Farm, which cultivates healthy minds.

WALK

DIANE'S TRAIL

1.5 miles (1:15 minutes)

Gould Farm, a community-based psychiatric rehabilitation center, is nearing a century of work. In 1992 Diane Rausch, wife of an employee, died of breast cancer. Her husband, Bob, and friends, developed a nature trail and bridge in her honor. Follow Route 23 to Monterey; turn south on Curtis Road, near the General Store. The trail begins at a kiosk on the left just after crossing the Konkapot River; parking is 150 yards farther, on the right, in front of a garage. Copies of a guide, keyed to numbers along the trail, are available at the kiosk.

The trail is blazed blue. Trail builders have worked hard to protect the wetlands with bog bridging. The recommended route follows a fence line from the kiosk to the large wooden footbridge over Rawson Brook and then along a property line to gravel Wellman Road. Turn right on the road, crossing the brook, to the trail entrance in an area still recovering from the tornado of 1995. The trail follows beside the brook, with lovely views of water and ridge, back to the kiosk. A spur on the far side of the bridge leads to the the confluence of Rawson and Konkapot, where a bench invites contemplation. The mix of lowland surrounding a meandering brook and slightly higher pine forest, together with open field, provides considerable variety.

GREAT BARRINGTON

Great Barrington became the focus for southern Berkshire—the shopping center for the hilltowns that surround it, home to a registry of deeds, a court, and other status symbols. Nowadays it boasts fine restaurants, a theater, bookstores, a college, and numerous other amenities. Along with the center of town, on Route 7, there is an old mill area at Housatonic, once home to the Rising Paper Company. Originally settled in 1726 at the Great Fordway on the Housatonic, which gave way to the Great Bridge, the town is also on the old Great Road from Boston to Albany (roughly Route 23 now), so it is no wonder that although named after Viscount Barrington, it magnified the name. By tradition, the Indian village that preceded the town was named Mahaiwe, or "place downstream." A venerable theater in town retains the name.

Back in the days when Americans and British were on the same side, General Jeffrey Amherst, on his way to Ticonderoga to defeat the French, camped with his troops

where the Great Road crossed the Green River. After sepa-
rating from Sheffield in 1761, the town became a seat of dis-
content with British rule. In August 1774, a group of men
seized the court house, preventing the King's Court from
holding session. Thus the town claims the "first open resist-
ance to British rule in America." Yet the town's residents
included many Tories—notably leading citizen David
Ingersoll, who was imprisoned in Litchfield, Connecticut,
and then exiled. British general John Burgoyne, marching in
defeat from Saratoga on the Great Road during the
Revolutionary War, was feted in Great Barrington; during
Shays's uprising of dissident veterans the courthouse was
once again seized.

William Cullen Bryant, this country's first native-born
poet, practiced law in Great Barrington. A poem of his told
of an unhappy Indian love affair culminating with her leap
from Squaw Peak on Monument Mountain, north of the
center of town. A more vivid attempt to explain the cairn or
stone pile by the trail records that when the Indian maiden
hurled herself from the summit, she caught hold of a branch
on the way down and remained suspended for two days,
howling all the while, until a lightning bolt struck the tree,
dropping both maiden and branch to oblivion. Her Mahican
Indian relatives built the cairn in her memory, to which
passersby continue to add stones.

In a different application of electricity, William Stanley
tested his theory of alternating current by providing street
lighting for his home town, the first commercial use of electric current. The Housatonic Agricultural Society and its
successors held summer fairs at the Barrington Fairgrounds
beginning in 1842.

Camping

The nearest campground is at Benedict Pond, Beartown
State Forest, east on Route 23 to forest HQ. Follow the signs
along Blue Hill Road from there. The parking fee is modest.
Lifeguards protect the swimming beach in season. At

Monument Mountain, Route 7 north of town, the picnic grove (910 feet in elevation) is a lovely, shaded spot.

WALKS

RIVER WALK

Two short sections

This project required enormous removal of trash and great labor in trail construction. As leader Rachel Fletcher says, "I don't think of it as 2,500 feet long, I think of it as 1,700 volunteers long." River Walk, since 1988, has rallied Great Barrington citizens to clean up the section of the Housatonic River that flows through town and to reclaim the banks from generations of industrial waste and neglect. It is ongoing.

Enter between Riverbank House and Brooks Drugs, where a bulletin board informs you of the labor and the people. Descend the steps to the trail proper and follow downstream for the equivalent of about a block, passing a piece of sculpture through which runoff flows and a memorial bench. The river stands revealed, its banks stabilized and native trees and other vegetation planted.

Enter the second section from the large parking lot at the end of Church Street, first exploring the W. E. B. DuBois River Garden, both a water garden and a native species garden. The stones around the latter are the major native examples. The trail, which includes a canoe launch, runs both upstream past the Berkshire Corporation and downstream to Bridge Street, where a memorial rises to a battle in King Philip's War.

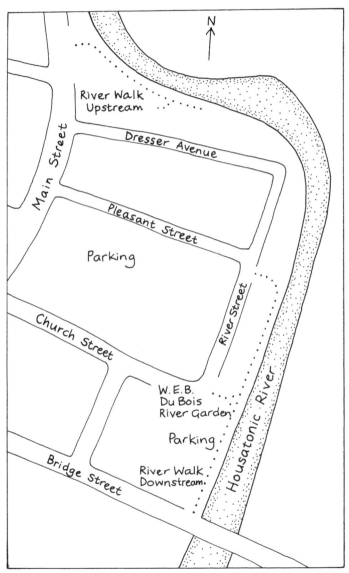

GREAT BARRINGTON: RIVER WALK

SEEKONK

Great Barrington and Alford, 3 or 6 miles (1.5 or 2.5 hours)

Either two short or one long hike can be enjoyed on the east side of town and into Alford. Drive up Taconic Street at St. James Church, which becomes Alford Road after curving right. Follow Alford Road downhill past Simon's Rock College and then, soon, bear left on Seekonk Road where the walk begins.

Park carefully by the small bridge. Most of these roads are gravel. Walk south on Round Hill Road, looking out from high farms. Turn right on Seekonk Cross Road and then either right on Seekonk back to the beginning or left on Green River Road, right on North Egremont Road, right on Cross Road, and right again on Seekonk Cross Road. Go left on Seekonk to the beginning. (The brook in these parts is known alternately as Alford or Seekonk.) This is a fine rolling stroll or bicycle ride with lovely panoramic views.

BENEDICT POND

1.5 miles (45 minutes) for shorter loop

Another walk can be reached from Great Barrington's Monument Valley Road. Coming south on Route 7, turn left just beyond the high school. Turn left on Stony Brook Road, which becomes Blue Hill Road. A bicycling expedition from Monument Valley Road is 12 miles. Turn left to Benedict Pond to walk a longer or shorter circuit. There is a small parking fee in season. Bikers will want to do a 3.5-mile road trip around Benedict Pond. Walkers can circumambulate on a 1.5-mile trail, blazed blue. This fine swimming area, presided over by lifeguards, is available for walkers who wish to swim, together with changing rooms and outhouses. The pond is lovely; the woods and cliffs behind, dramatic.

The AT passes through Beartown State Forest, with a shelter south of Mount Wilcox, which the AT does not

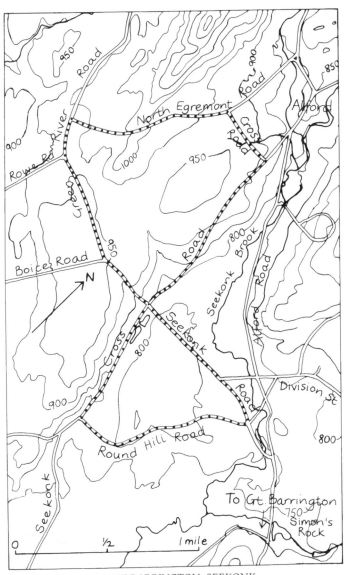

GREAT BARRINGTON: SEEKONK

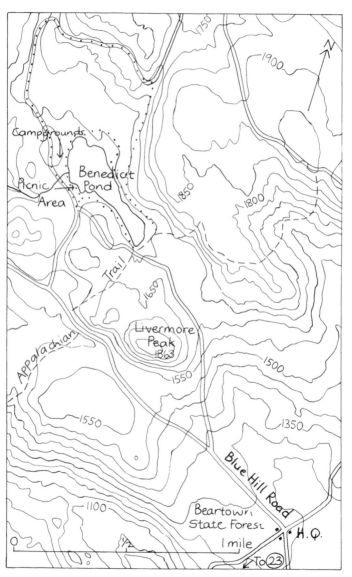

GREAT BARRINGTON: BENEDICT POND

climb. That peak rises 2,112 feet, without much of a view because the lookout tower is closed. It is a relatively easy climb (4 miles round trip) from the pond. Beartown is busy in the winter with snowmobiles and cross-country skiers.

HIKE

MONUMENT MOUNTAIN

3 miles (1.5 hour hiking time)

Road approaches

Monument Mountain is a pillar of stones, unmistakable to the motorist on Route 7, just north of the center of the town of Great Barrington, a few miles south of Stockbridge, and slightly south of Monument Mountain Regional High School. Of the several parking lots on the west side of the road, the one at the picnic grounds (with the green Trustees of Reservations sign) is handiest for the hike described here.

MONUMENT MOUNTAIN

TTOR maintains this 503-acre reservation (and asks you to make a contribution if you hike it). This pile of stones has a largely clear ridge, giving you a good look at Beartown State Forest to the east, the Taconic Range to the west, and the valleys in between. If it isn't a tradition at the regional high school below the mountain for seniors to hike to the summit, it ought to be. This is less of a wilderness hike than others in this guide: from the summit, you can look directly into a former landfill operation and onto the whizzing vehicles of Route 7, as well as the panorama of unspoiled land. As always, it depends where you choose to look.

Although not lengthy, this is a steep, rugged climb. It is also a storied one. In 1850, a publisher arranged an outing for several writers on this mountain: Herman Melville, Nathaniel Hawthorne, and Oliver Wendell Holmes. The account of the wagon loaded with picnic goods, including champagne, and the liveried servants who accompanied them, may make you question how they made it up the trail. You will find out.

The well-trod trail, which is blazed white, leaves from the north corner of the parking lot, near a large map. It is moderately steep, passing through hemlocks, with scree (rocky rubble at the bottom of a slope) on the left. A trail enters right in five minutes. In a quarter hour, faced with a ravine, you swing left. Ignore all other trails, many of which are detours, keeping to the left. The stream on the right flows in lovely waterfalls in the spring. In places the trail is badly eroded, although the Trustees have labored hard at stone water bars, to try to deflect the freshets.

Turn left again at 22 minutes, on the trail to Squaw Peak. Almost immediately you pass a rock with the year the (then-called) Trustees of Public Reservations acquired the first portion of the property: 1899. The trail is quite steep, soon requiring clambering over quartzite boulders. The lookout left seems to be directly over the school. You are on the summit ridge in half an hour, but persevere, through the pitch pine, to the peak that honors an Indian maid, thought, at least by the poet, to have flung herself to her death. Pay attention to your footing, which is rough. The rocks themselves, with their lichens, are intriguing. One impending rock has the date 1888 carved in it, albeit painted over by more recent visitors. You may wish to push farther to Devil's Pulpit (marked by a scenic vista sign) and continue to the return trail.

For better footing and a more leisurely trip follow back the way you came until turning left just beyond the inscribed boulder. Note you are on more of a road; indeed, the old carriage road up which the literary party came. Suddenly you sense something has changed. Consider: you hear more birds, not necessarily because they are louder but because you have rounded a corner of the cobble, leaving the state highway traffic noises behind you. Again, keep left as various trails enter. The going is much more gradual than

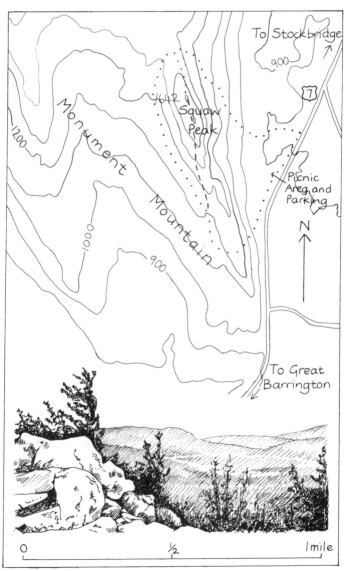

To Stockbridge

900

7

1642 Squaw Peak

Monument Mountain

1200

1000

900

Picnic Area and Parking

N

To Great Barrington

0   ½   1 mile

GREAT BARRINGTON: MONUMENT MOUNTAIN

on the way up. The hemlocks are larger. Even bigger are the boulders that have tumbled down the steep sides in this romantic spot.

Gradually you begin to hear the road sounds again, as you work around the south end of the mountain. An obscured trail, left, leads along a stone wall to the cairn. The relatively newly cut trail takes you parallel with Route 7, north to the picnic ground, which you reach after 1:17 walking time—not counting the time you lingered at the summit.

TYRINGHAM

The Tyringham Valley remains one of the most lovely, bucolic views in Berkshire. It has stayed that way honestly. No railroad ever came through town, no interurban trolleys nor even a numbered highway. Like Williamstown, it is nearly surrounded by mountains, nestled between October Mountain and Beartown State Forests.

Settled in 1735, Tyringham has always been a farming community, although over the years it has had just a bite of many of the treats served up more extensively in other Berkshire towns. It is the only town in Massachusetts named after a woman, however: Jane Tyringham Beresford, colonial governor Bernard's cousin. A handful of Shakers settled here in 1792, growing to a community of 100, cultivating 1,500 acres by the mid-19th century when they began to fade. Their land was purchased to build an elaborate summer colony, known as Fernside, on Hop Brook.

Industry arrived in the 19th century, especially the Steadman Rake Company. Richard Watson Gilder, editor of *Scribner's* and later *Century* magazines, arrived in 1898 to build Four Brooks Farm, which attracted the literary and artistic notables of the day, from naturalist John Burroughs to sculptor Augustus Saint-Gaudens to historian and writer Henry Adams to humorist Mark Twain—all of whom summered there.

Tyringham town from Tyringham Cobble

Camping

Tyringham remains free of tourist trappings. There is a campsite, however, at Upper Goose Pond, for AT hikers, just over the line from Tyringham in Lee.

WALK

TYRINGHAM COBBLE

2 miles (1 hour)

Road approaches

To get to Tyringham from the Lee interchange of the Massachusetts Turnpike, at the junction of Route 20 jog briefly right on Route 102 west, then take Tyringham Road due south. Turn right at the town center on Jerusalem Road. Stay right where Church Street enters. Soon you will see a TTOR sign, right, just beyond a red barn. Park in the lot. Note the information in the kiosk and follow the trail along the fence.

TYRINGHAM COBBLE

Follow blue blazes into the woods. To make the loop clockwise, bear left at the main trail, which briefly coincides with the AT. The trail enters a wooded area and then comes out on a rocky outlook, the obvious picnic site. The white church and country town are picturesquely set against the wooded hillsides surrounding Goose Pond. The trail descends, through additional stiles, parallels the town's main street, and gradually swings right back to the trail junction. TTOR owns 206 acres, to which the trail provides an introduction.

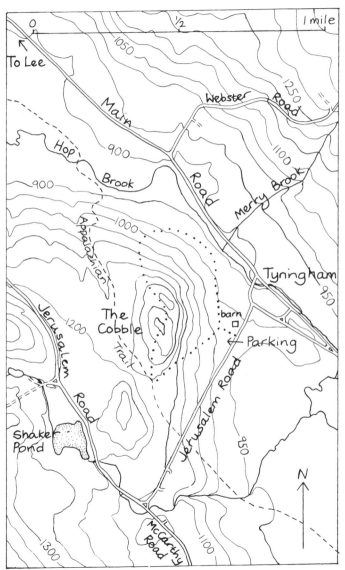

TYRINGHAM: TYRINGHAM COBBLE

STOCKBRIDGE

This 260-year-old town (incorporated in 1739) started out chartered by England's King George II to "the Housatannack Tribe of Indians . . . to their use and behoof forever." The Europeans who settled there had a notion they could improve the lot of the Indians, however, which led eventually—as it often did—to the Indians being driven out.

The Reverend John Sergeant, who took the trouble to learn the Mahican language, arrived as first missionary in 1734, teaching Chiefs Konkapot and Umpachene domestic skills like agriculture and house building. His true friendship attracted Indians from many miles away. Jonathan Edwards succeeded him. While well disposed to the native Americans, he was preoccupied with his religious writings and hectored by those Christian families sent to be worthy examples to the Indians, such as that of Ephraim Williams Sr. This worthy sold them liquor and connived to acquire their land. So the Indian village became the center of the European town. In 1783 the natives held their last campfire here and migrated to a reservation in western New York State and thence to Wisconsin.

When Judge Theodore Sedgwick moved to Stockbridge from Sheffield in 1785, he stamped the place an important and wealthy town. By the 1860s, like Lenox, it had become the country seat for many influential eastern families. It attracted artists, such as Daniel Chester French, who designed the seated Lincoln in the Lincoln Memorial, and Norman Rockwell, the magazine illustrator. It planned well, creating the Laurel Hill Association in 1835, the first village improvement organization in this country, and saving its most precious buildings and historic sites. The Laurel Hill Association is still active, meeting annually, its members planting trees and maintaining trails.

Several of the early and staunch (European) families— the Sergeants, Woodbridges, Williamses, Dwights, Stoddards, Edwardses, Sedgwicks, Fields, Butlers, Choates, Parsonses, Rathbuns, Guerrieris, and Burghardts—still have scions in town or nearby. Seven U.S. ambassadors have lived here. So have Cyrus Field, who laid the Atlantic cable, and his equally remarkable brothers. Three men educated here sat on the U.S. Supreme Court at the same time: Henry Billings Brown, Stephen J. Field, and David Joshua Brewer. Its recent residents also include the famous and respected, such as psychoanalyst Erik Erikson and theologian Reinhold Niebuhr. And of course one day in the 1960s, according to the song, Officer Obie arrested Arlo Guthrie for throwing some trash from Alice's Restaurant by a Stockbridge roadside, which Arlo spun into an antiwar song and movie.

The town center, which looks like . . . well, a Norman Rockwell *Saturday Evening Post* cover, is the most choked by summer tourists of any Berkshire town. People park a mile out along all the highways to visit the Indian Mission House (the actual building, although not in its original location), Naumkeag (the Choate mansion, now, like the Mission House, under the care of TTOR), the many upscale shops and, at the center of things, the Red Lion Inn. A bit farther out, you will find the Berkshire Theatre Festival, Chesterwood (the sculptor's home), the Berkshire Botanical Garden, and, at the north end of town, the Norman Rockwell Museum, Stockbridge Bowl, and Tanglewood (summer home of the Boston Symphony Orchestra).

WALKS

ICE GLEN

3.5 miles or shorter (1.5 hours)

Strolls in Stockbridge are legion and lovely, not to mention the fact that summer and early fall biking or even walking is speedier than automobiling. The Laurel Hill Association publishes a Hike and Bike Guide, available at the town hall or library, with a useful set of maps.

Start with the Ice Glen, maintained by the Laurel Hill

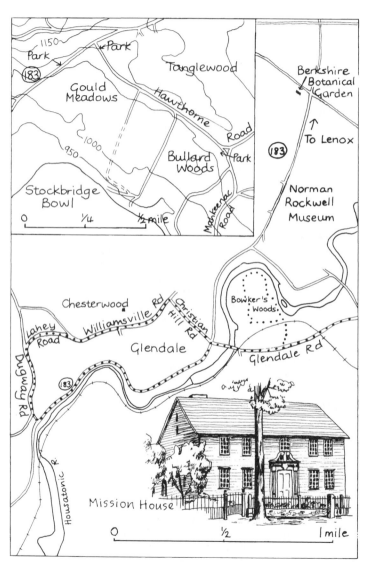

1150
Park
183
Park
Tanglewood
Gould
Meadows
Hawthorne
Road
Berkshire
Botanical
Garden
1000
950
Bullard
Woods
Park
183
To Lenox
Stockbridge
Bowl
Mahkeenac
Road
Norman
Rockwell
Museum
0   ¼   ½ mile

Chesterwood
Williamsville Rd
Christian
Hill Rd
Bowker's
Woods
Lahey
Road
Williamsville
Glendale
Glendale Rd
Dugway
Rd
183
Housatonic R.
Mission House
0   ½   1 mile

STOCKBRIDGE: SEVERAL WALKS

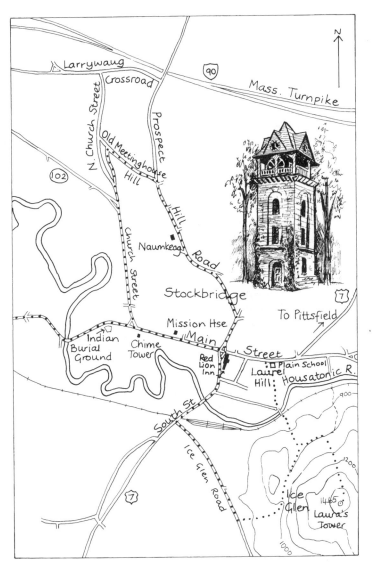

STOCKBRIDGE: SEVERAL WALKS

Association. Beginning at the Red Lion Inn, walk south .5 mile on Route 7 to Ice Glen Road, beyond the bridge. Follow this small lane for .5 mile. Turn left up a shared private drive and the trail. (It would be possible to do a two-car walk, but little parking is available on Ice Glen Road.) The blue-and/or-yellow-blazed trail, although short, is rough, in spite of noble efforts to ease the way over boulders and around large, prone hemlocks. It gets its name from the fact that ice lasts longer in the stony crevasse than anywhere else around. Occasionally on Halloween the town stages a scary parade through the glen, a tradition going back 100 years.

After climbing 100 feet through the tangled glen and reading the carving in the cliff crediting David Dudley Field Jr. for donating the property to the town, you can turn right to ascend via numerous switchbacks another 465 feet in elevation to Laura's Tower. The steel tower at the top, on a clear day, gives a fine view of the Berkshire Hills from Mount Everett and Race Mountain to Mount Greylock, not to mention downtown Stockbridge. A compass rose labels the sights. Descend from the tower as you came up, but turn right on the main trail, cross the Memorial Footbridge, and head back to town by Park and South Streets. Total mileage, starting at the Red Lion and including Laura's Tower: 3.5 miles.

To avoid the rough section through the glen and shorten the trip, start on the Memorial Footbridge side, climb to the tower, and return. You can find a trail behind the Plain School or walk out Park Street.

BOWKER'S WOODS

.5 mile (15 minutes)

A short trail passes near the loop in the Housatonic and across the freight line and old interurban trolley right-of-way to give you a look at Bowker's Woods. To get there, go west on Main Street from the Red Lion Inn, continue straight at the Chime Tower, past the Indian Burial Ground on a knoll to the left, cross the river and bear right up the hill and out Glendale Road to a discreet opening in the stone wall, right, for the Lower Trail (1.5 miles from the inn, not included in mileage). This is an easy and pleasant stroll, passing along a bluff by the river with lovely views. To get to the Upper Trail, which winds through some lovely pines, bear right twice after crossing the river, following Glendale North Road to Route 183. Jog right and left, just beyond a small pond, for the entrance to the trail.

PROSPECT HILL

3 miles (1 hour)

A fine route for stroll or bike takes you up Prospect Hill and back on Church Street. Begin directly across Main Street from the Red Lion Inn, on Pine Street. Pass the tennis courts, then bear left on Prospect Hill Road and continue up to Naumkeag, the James H. Choate home designed in 1885 by Stanford White. Swing left on Old Meetinghouse Hill Road, beyond, and thence by Field Street (gravel) back to Church Street, getting a look at the attractive backside of Naumkeag on your way to the Chime Tower, where you turn left for the inn.

The Marian Fathers, across the road from Naumkeag, allow walkers on their extensive grounds, for an alternative route, or you can extend the trip by a mile by continuing up Prospect Hill to Larrywaug Road and then down North Church Street.

GLENDALE

Several alternatives

Another set of walks and bike rides lies to the west and a bit south of Stockbridge in the village of Glendale. From the Red Lion Inn in Stockbridge follow Main Street west by the Town Hall, Chime Tower, and the Indian Burial Ground and across the river to Glendale Road, past the entrance to Bowker's Woods Lower Trail and south on Castle Hill Road. Turn left on Cherry Hill Road and left again on Cherry Street to the beginning (3 miles). You might also venture farther out Glendale Road, by auto perhaps, across the railroad tracks and over the river a second time to Route 183. Park at the Glendale Post Office and walk straight ahead up a short, steep section of Christian Hill Road to gravel Williamsville Road. Turn left. Soon on your right is Chesterwood, once the home of sculptor Daniel Chester French and now a National Trust museum. Bear right at the fork to Dugway Road, also gravel. Turn left there, along Mohawk Lake Brook to Route 183 and along the river, past the restored hydroelectric plant, and back to the point of origin. Although Route 183 winds charmingly along the Housatonic, vehicles here travel too fast. Use caution or avoid Route 183 by retracing your footsteps.

GOULD MEADOWS AND BULLARD WOODS

Various options

Neither of these lovely properties has a trail system but both are open to the public for wandering. Both are off Hawthorne Road, paralleling the northern side of Stockbridge Bowl. (Note: Hawthorne Street, confusingly, is perpendicular to Hawthorne Road and heads toward Lenox.) There is a map at the Gould Meadows parking area, a few hundred yards down Route 183 from Hawthorne Road (you are near Tanglewood, to the north, and near the site, to the south, of the canoe portion of the Great Josh Billings Runaground, held annually in the fall). The higher land provides a remarkable view of the Bowl and excellent picnicking. Carry out any trash, please. You can wander down to the water if you like.

Bullard Woods is cited by state foresters as the best place in the county to see large trees. A scruffy field at the corner of Hawthorne Street and Road provides parking; if you look carefully you will see a sign at the edge of the field. Logging roads curve through the 50-acre stand of enormous oaks, especially along the edge of the meadow. Other large trees include sugar maples; shagbark hickory; large tulip poplar, including one about 4 feet in circumference, with a faded sign attached; and many large white pines—including one 18 feet in circumference, barred from being a record because it appears to have been formed when two trees grew together. Stumps in the woods show where chestnuts were cut in response to the blight (pre-1920).

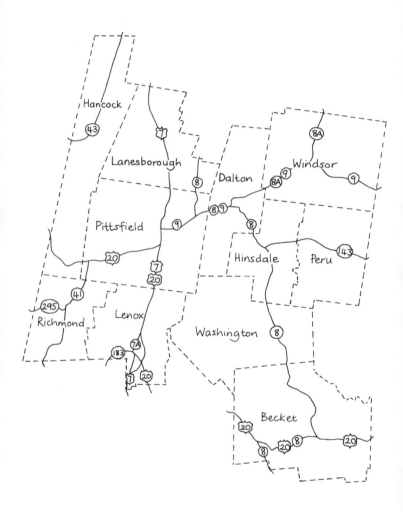

CENTRAL COUNTY

CENTRAL COUNTY

LENOX

Lenox is not at all what you see from Route 7, a strip of shops and restaurants. The old center of town is on Route 7A; that, too, has a touristy inclination but is recognizable as a community with a rich history.

Originally connected to the outside world only by an Indian path that followed the Housatonic River, Yokuntown was first settled in 1750, named after Chief Yokun, a Stockbridge Indian. When the town was incorporated, in 1767, it was named for Charles Lennox, Duke of Richmond. At some time, one *n* was deemed sufficient; the opposite of the inclination that added "great" to Viscount Barrington's name. Considered a home to Tories during the Revolutionary War, by early in the 19th century Lenox boasted thriving industries that led it to replace Great Barrington as the shire town: hence the courthouse (1816), now the Lenox Library. Pittsfield usurped the county seat in 1868.

Lenox changed utterly, however, when Charles Sedgwick moved there in 1821. Shortly thereafter, his sister, writer Catharine Sedgwick, joined him. Together they hosted the literary lights of the day and inspired other families to build great estates in town, the so-called cottages designed on the Newport, Rhode Island, model. Many well-to-do gentry from New York and Boston developed large estates in and around Lenox, tastefully tucking their enormous homes out of sight behind shrubbery. Few of these remain in private hands now. The most famous visitor at the time was the British actress Fanny Kemble, who charmed

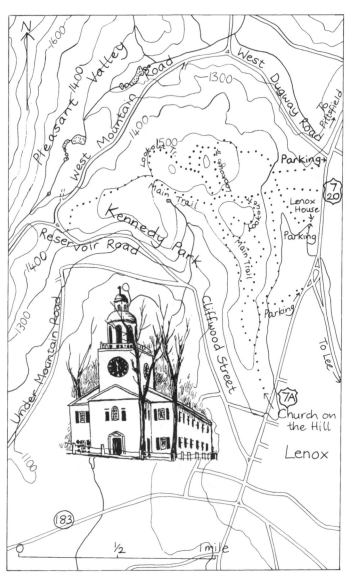

LENOX: KENNEDY PARK

the community and to whom Longfellow addressed a son-
net. She donated the proceeds of a reading to pay for the
clock in the tower of Lenox's lovely Church on the Hill.

WALKS

KENNEDY PARK

3–4 miles (1.5 hours)

A history of large estates—as opposed to farm land,
cutover land, or developed land—has left some of the
largest trees in the county in Lenox and Stockbridge, as you
can see in Bullard Woods or driving through these fashion-
able towns. One gorgeous glimpse of the kind of land that
is not recently grown-over farm fields is Lenox's 502-acre
Kennedy Park.The town has created new entrance near the
junction of West Dugway Road and Routes 7 and 20, with a
16-car parking lot, picnic area, and handicapped-accessible
trail loop. Of course it is still possible to get onto the trails
from the gate near the Church on the Hill.

The area was the site of the Aspinwall Hotel, built in
1902 to accommodate the wealthy who wanted to visit their
cottage-dwelling friends. The hotel burned in 1931 and its
grounds became the John D. Kennedy Park in 1957. The
main trail, blazed white, breeds numerous offshoots, so
that you can design your own route, consulting the map
near the entrance. One possibility includes the Lookout
Trail, blazed red. In combination, red and white give you an
invigorating stroll.

RESERVOIRS

Lenox and Richmond, 8 miles or less (3 hours or less)

A pleasant and lengthy walk begins outside Pleasant
Valley, the Audubon wildlife sanctuary on West Mountain
Road, heading west. West Mountain Road becomes

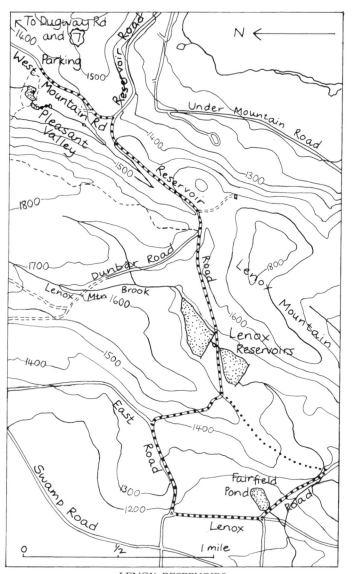

LENOX: RESERVOIRS

Reservoir Road, passing Upper Root Reservoir (right) and then quite small Large Reservoir (left). At the fork, follow Reservoir Road right and then left. You are in the town of Richmond now, once a part of Yokuntown but split off when the Bay Colony sold the tracts of "Indian Land." Keep straight where Lenox Road enters right and bear left with it around Fairfield Pond (about 4 miles). The next left turn will return you to Large Reservoir, whence you can follow Reservoir and West Roads back to your point of departure. Some remarkable homes jut out of swiftly falling hillsides. En route you will see also wooded and pasture land. Variations are available by taking different turns. This is also a good bicycle route, with even more variations than for hiking, depending on ambition.

HIKE

PLEASANT VALLEY/LENOX MOUNTAIN

3 miles (1.5 hours hiking time)

Road approaches

Pleasant Valley Wildlife Sanctuary is off the Lenox-Pittsfield Road (Routes 7 and 20). Turn west on West Dugway Road, at the sanctuary sign, north of the junction with Route 7A but south of the junction of Holmes Road. Follow Dugway, a blacktopped road, a mile until it ends at West Mountain Road. Bear left on this gravel road for .8 mile. The sanctuary has parking lots on both sides of the road. It is closed on Mondays.

Rest rooms are available in the barn. Maps and other interesting pamphlets are available at the window, where nonmembers of Massachusetts Audubon will be asked to pay a small fee for use of the sanctuary. There are no shelters or camping areas on this hike. Incidentally, no dogs are allowed on this property. Cross-country skiing is not allowed. Collecting of plants, of course, is not allowed; nor is it on any public lands or most private lands.

The Pleasant Valley Wildlife Sanctuary, one of three Massachusetts Audubon properties in the county, was established in 1929. Seven miles of trails wind through 1,100 acres of Berkshire uplands and beaver swamps. A trailside museum is open mid-May through October.

PLEASANT VALLEY/LENOX MOUNTAIN

This is a lovely short hike, relatively steep, with a rewarding view from the summit of Lenox Mountain. Other strategic lookouts along the trail survey the surroundings. At least in the spring, trails follow delightful brooks with sparkling waterfalls.

From the Audubon administration building follow the main trail, past the barn on the left and the activity center on the right. From this spot you can see the destination: the tower on the ridge to the west. The Bluebird Trail passes through fields that are beginning to fill in with second growth. Audubon is displaying the way first weeds replace grass, bushes replace weeds, and gradually trees fill in former farm-land. In this area, pines come to shield out undergrowth, and then, finally, hardwoods take over from the pines.

Follow straight ahead as two trails depart to the right. At the sanctuary all trails heading away from the administra-tion building are blazed blue; all returning to the center are blazed yellow. Cross trails are blazed white. It is difficult to get lost.

At the bottom of the slope, cross a bridge over Yokun Brook under a stand of tall pines, leave a beaver swamp on the right, and cross a second bridge (at 8 minutes), follow-ing signs to the tower at various intersections. The trail con-tinues up the brook you just crossed. (You may want to detour on alternate trails to examine the industrious beavers' activities.)

At the four-way intersection (12 minutes), go straight. The brook is on the left. As you gain elevation, laurel, which blossoms in June, begins to fill in under hardwood trees. You pass out of the sanctuary land into Lenox watershed

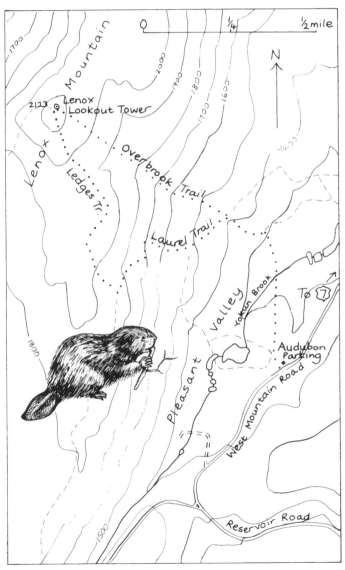

LENOX: PLEASANT VALLEY/LENOX MOUNTAIN

lands, but Audubon maintains trails throughout. The trail weaves back and forth across the brook, which runs in the spring with several falls. Large hemlocks aim to the sky in the ravines and along the ledges. The schist over which the water runs contains quartz outcroppings. At 30 minutes the trail begins to skirt a ledge, left. In 40 minutes you come out on the summit.

The view from the summit looks down onto Richmond Pond, which seems to be very close, in spite of the 2,126 feet of elevation. (You have climbed 786 feet from the office.) The Catskill Mountains rise in the southwest. The Taconic highlands to the northwest are in Pittsfield State Forest. Lake Onota lies to the west-northwest. Looking east you see the highlands of October Mountain State Forest. To the southeast you look down into the extremely pleasant valley. The tower adds some 80 feet of up to the view.

Follow the Ledges Trail to the southeast rather than the jeep road. Remember, returning trails are blazed yellow. In four minutes you begin to pass over more ledges, descending and climbing along the ridge. At 1:02 from the administration building you come to a trail junction at Fairview, which gives another nice look into the sanctuary's 670 acres. Turn left on the aptly named Laurel Trail, which begins a steep descent partly in an intermittent streambed. The hardwoods now include oak, birch, and beech.

At 1:15 go straight at the intersection with the Ravine Trail. At 1:19, bear right at a familiar four corners. You are now back on the trail you began climbing, appropriately known as Overbrook. Although you have been traversing rocky outcroppings, the valley lies atop limestone, buffering the effects of acid rain and affording hospitable conditions for certain ferns and other rare species. Bear right at the Y. At 1:24 cross the first bridge and at 1:30 minutes pass the administration building.

The sanctuary map shows numerous other strolls and hikes, the one to the tower being the most rigorous. You could spend a full day walking through this beautifully maintained property and enjoying a picnic. Massachusetts

Audubon organizes many educational activities, including cross-country skiing and snowshoeing at Canoe Meadows, another Berkshire sanctuary, located a few miles north, off Holmes Road in Pittsfield (see the decription below).

RICHMOND

So near and yet so far. While a noisy Sunday afternoon Tanglewood traffic jam has clogged the roads through neighboring Lenox and nearby Stockbridge, just over the mountain is silent and almost forgotten Richmond, enjoying its emptiness. This is a town without a center, but it does have fine roads to walk and places to visit.

WALKS

EAST ROAD

4.6 miles or less (2 hours)

Road approaches

From West Stockbridge take Pittsfield Road, which shortly becomes Swamp Road, heading north (at your start in the village, be careful not to confuse Pittsfield/Swamp Roads with Route 41). Go a little over 2 miles to the Lenox Road where you turn right and then park after driving in 100 yards or so. Park carefully: there is no official lot. East Road departs obliquely to the left, rising.

From Tanglewood: pass the main gate on Route 183, going south, and veer right, up the Richmond Mountain Road, passing Apple Tree Inn right. After climbing through several twisty turns, ignore a left turn on top of the mountain and descend toward Richmond on what, by now, is called Lenox Road. At the bottom of the hill, pass a pond right, then curve right, leading to East Road. Park more or less immediately, safely off the pavement, turn around, and walk up.

EAST ROAD

The mountains and valley along Swamp Road, from West Stockbridge up through Richmond, are sparsely populated and lovely. The walk on East Road (mostly gravel) is a stroll from and to nowhere in particular, although if you were ambitious, you could make a loop of it as explained below. Here's a simple out-and-back on East Road: the views of enormous farm fields and the Taconic Hills to the west are interestingly different when walking in each direction. Because the mountain rises sharply on the east side of this walk, if you want sunshine, hold off until midday. Sunsets from here are dramatic.

The walk to the other end of East Road, at Swamp Road, is as long, short, slow, or fast as you like. An estimated 2.3 miles takes you to Swamp Road, and so the full round trip is about 4.6 miles. The last part of East Road is in a woodsy residential area with some sweet country homes but no views. One highly unusual dome house can be seen about halfway out, right. You may want to walk only until the views disappear, then turn around to head back. You can picnic at roadside by the farm fields, but there are no facilities.

To make a loop: turn left on Swamp Road at the end of East Road, and head south to Lenox Road, where you turn left again and spy your waiting car. Add 2 miles.

STEVENS GLEN

2 miles (45 minutes)

Road approaches

Take Route 183 south from the center of Lenox. Turn right up the hill at the fork just beyond and across from Tanglewood's main gate. After passing Olivia's Outlook at the summit, turn left down a road marked Lenox Branch. Approximately .75 mile down the hill avail yourself of a

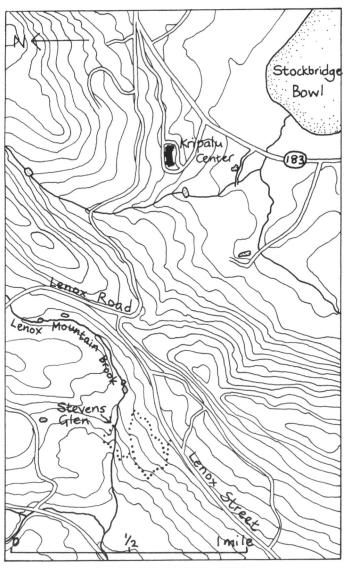

RICHMOND: STEVENS GLEN

parking pull-off at the trailhead, on the right, the first of two. The trail departs from the first, which has wooden guard rails. A sign says, tersely: "S. Glen."

STEVENS GLEN

Lenox Mountain Brook drops 100 feet through the rock walls of the glen, a romantic sight 120 years ago, when farmer Romanza Stevens charged visitors 25 cents to visit his attraction. He built a dance pavilion at the site, which attracted 900 on one 1913 evening. Today a visit is free, due to the generosity of the Pryor family, who donated the land to the Berkshire Natural Resources Council in 1995. It is still a romantic sight/site.

A spur from a loop trail leads to a platform that provides the best view. The trails, blazed red, descend 320 feet. After crossing some scraggily second growth, you arrive at a combination sign, map dispenser, and donation box. Turn right for a more leisurely, less steep descent; left for a more direct, steeper way. Following left, cross under utility lines and turn left on the spur before the bridge (12 minutes). You're in a shaded area of large hemlocks. Cross a bridge over a smaller water course that parallels Lenox Mountain Brook, then a larger bridge over the brook, which provides a nice view in itself. Stone steps lead up steeply to metal steps that take you to the viewing platform (18 minutes), with suitable safety warnings. The alternative route loops the opposite direction.

PERU

Peru is the highest town, in terms of elevation, in the county (and therefore the state), at 2,064 feet. It was incorporated July 4, 1771, as Partridgefield, because Oliver Partridge was one of the original purchasers of the grant. It began as a stop on a Boston-to-Albany stage line. The town was renamed in 1806, just two years after its western end had been lopped off to become Hinsdale because, like the country of Peru, it is in the mountains. And like the other Berkshire hilltowns, it subsisted on thin-soiled agriculture and a few mills, until young people heard of the kind of soil they grew out west. Then as now, residents went down to work in the more urban area of Pittsfield. With a population of under 821 and no shopping center, it remains one of the smallest Berkshire County towns. Few accommodations are available.

A 300-acre sanctuary near the center of town provides some excellent strolling.

WALK

RICE SANCTUARY

Various trails available

Road approaches

Take Route 8 to Hinsdale; turn east on Route 143 to the center of Peru, recognizable because of the church on the left and the road junction. Turn right on South Road for .8 mile, then right again on Rice Road.

DOROTHY FRANCES RICE SANTUARY

The sign welcomes you to the Dorothy Frances Rice Sanctuary, provided you arrive during daylight hours from May 28 to October 12. Local people also ski there in the winter. The small building is a visitors' center. Nearby most of the trails come together, their arrows color coded, at a busy sign. Choose your color and follow in the direction of the arrow, because some of the trees are blazed only on one side, often with colored blocks of wood. If you go the "wrong" way you won't see any blazes—although, for that matter, the trails are easy to follow, some sections even mowed.

Dorothy Frances Rice died of tuberculosis shortly after

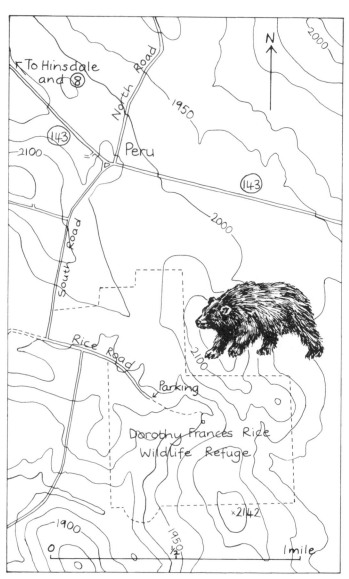

PERU: RICE SANCTUARY

Trail heads, Rice Sanctuary

graduating from Smith College, in Northampton. She loved this site of the family summer home. After her father, architect Orville Rice of New York City, died, her mother, Mary Rice, set up a trust to maintain the 300-acre property named for her daughter. The family home partly burned and was partly chewed down by voracious porcupines.

People in Peru still talk about two Smith College girls who lived in the visitors' center for one or more summers while studying the plants and animals. Eventually the trust turned the property over to the New England Forestry Foundation, together with an endowment. In season, a caretaker comes for two days a week to maintain the trails and the building. Mel Fassell of Pittsfield was caretaker of the property for a stretch of 25 years.

Although as many as 1,500 people a year wander through the sanctuary, you probably won't see any of them. For the most part, the trails pass through old field growth laced with stone walls. The lengths of the walks vary and, of course, it is possible to connect them in different ways as they cross each other. Figure on 30 minutes to an hour— more if you want. Yes, those are bear scratches on the shed, for the Peru wilderness is alive with fauna as well as flora.

CHESTER

Although this walk begins on a gravel road in Chester, east of Becket, south of Peru, and therefore in Hampden County, the trail itself is in Middlefield, Hampshire County, adjacent to Berkshire County. If that confuses, it may help to know you pass close by the tri-county marker.

WALK

THE KEYSTONE ARCHES

Middlefield Road to 70-foot bridge and back, 3 miles (1.5 hours)

Alexander Birnie built 10 arches in 1839-40, the first keystone arch railroad bridges in this country, to get the Western Railroad through the Westfield River Valley and up the Becket hills. Some of the bridges have been replaced or avoided by altering the rail route. George Washington Whistler, the painter's father, engineered this feat and then went on to design the Trans-Siberian Railroad. All the stone was laid up dry and still is without mortar. On this walk you get a look at a double arch bridge, still in use; a 65-foot high abandoned bridge; pick and shovel rock cuts and retaining wall; and a 70-foot high abandoned bridge. As the trail leads to two bridges, parents and pet-owners should note that there are no fences or guard rails. The CSX line on the far side of the river is still in use. The land belongs to Massachusetts Fisheries and Wildlife, so it is open for hunting.

Turn off Route 20 onto the Middlefield Road in the center of Chester. Follow 2.5 miles to parking on the left on the unmarked Herbert Cross Road. Look left to see the double arch bridge. Some trucks belonging to the railroad and off-road vehicles use this road, which soon crosses a tributary on a steel grate bridge. Another parking area is just before the bridge; this is the farthest it is reasonable to drive in a road vehicle. An attractive small cascade is just above the bridge. The route is blazed blue. Follow the road to the second right (at a foundation); and then right again, into the woods on the trail proper. At an intersection of trails, go straight across the brook in spite of an earth berm. You climb and then descend. The way that soon enters left is a section of the Old Pontoosuc Turnpike, the stage road to Albany 100 years older than the railroad. You will be able to

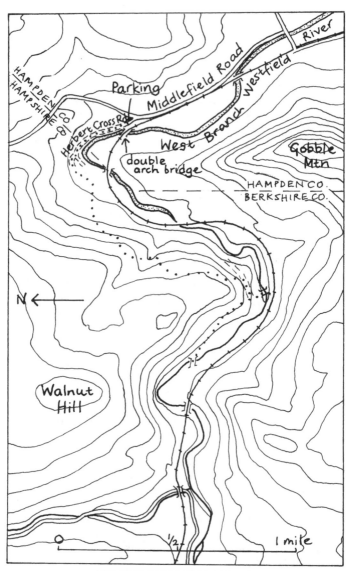

CHESTER: KEYSTONE ARCHES

pick out other sections of it. You meet the former rail line and turn left to check out the 65-foot arch; then double back along the right of way to see—look down—the stone retaining wall and the cuts. You pass an old signal stand and end on a bridge 70 feet over the river.

A great idea for the adventuresome would be to carry an inner tube on the way in and to float out.

PITTSFIELD

Solomon and Sarah Deming arrived from Wethersfield, Connecticut, at what is presently Elm Street and built their first home in 1752. They were Pontoosuc's first European settlers and their daughter, Dorothy, the first child of European extraction born in this wilderness. The other earliest residents were also from Connecticut, which was true in much of western Massachusetts. Settlers gathered in sufficient numbers over the next year to discuss founding a town and building a meeting house, located beside what became Park Square. They decided to name the town for William Pitt, the English statesman who befriended the colonies and whose birthday was the same as the day in April 1761 that Berkshire County split off from Hampshire County. Pittsfield was to become the shire town or county seat of Berkshire.

In 1764, the Reverend Thomas Allen became the first minister, later accompanying the troops to the Battle of Bennington (1777) as the "Fighting Parson." The elm next to the first meeting house was spared in the construction of the second church, the one Charles Bulfinch designed, by the intercession of Lucretia Williams. Loyal to the king like her father, Israel Williams, she married the ardent patriot John Williams (no relation; every fourth person in western Massachusetts in those days was named Williams). Yet she survived and their marriage survived. At least they had plenty to talk about and, in 1783, when the peace was signed, they threw a party that, judging from contemporary accounts, may scarcely have been equaled since.

The elm, although struck by lightning, lived into the days Herman Melville spent in Pittsfield. He described scarred Captain Ahab in terms of that tree, "greenly alive but branded." It finally had to be removed in 1864.

Poet Oliver Wendell Holmes's great-grandfather, Jacob Wendell, who originally bought the land for Pittsfield in 1736, drove a wonderful "one-hoss shay," subject of the poem "The Deacon's Masterpiece." That shay is stored in the basement of the Berkshire Museum, on South Street, together with many other artifacts from the city's literary, historic, natural, and artistic past. O. W. Holmes's property is now owned by the Massachusetts Audubon Society, called, as it always has been, Canoe Meadows. It is located where Pomeroy Avenue meets Holmes Road: Holmes Road being also the address of Melville's Pittsfield home, "Arrowhead"—now the headquarters of the Berkshire County Historical Society. The poet Henry Wadsworth Longfellow, of *Hiawatha* fame, stayed at the Dutch Colonial mansion built in 1781 by Henry Van Schaack, now the Pittsfield Country Club.

This building on Route 7, south of town, originally known as Broad Hall, was also the home for nine years of Elkanah Watson, who married science with agriculture in Berkshire. The merino sheep he imported changed the nature of farming in the county; the agricultural fairs he founded still continue in some form or other throughout western Massachusetts.

Another application of science created the modern city, which in the 19th century was smaller than its North County rival, North Adams. In 1907 the General Electric Company established its plant in Pittsfield. A city that took 150 years to gain a population of 25,000 doubled that in the next 30 years. (And continued growing to near 58,000 in 1960. It has declined since.)

Early industries used water for paper and power. As well as drawing from the Housatonic River and its tributaries, industries enlarged two lakes, Onota and Pontoosuc, as reservoirs. Both now serve as recreational bases. Public swimming is available at Burbank Park on Onota and at the park just off Route 7 on Hancock Road for Pontoosuc. A city of nearly 46,000, 36 percent of the entire county, Pittsfield is refreshed by its lakes and keeps its eye on the hills that surround it.

WALKS

DOWNTOWN

8 blocks (30 minutes)

Most of the walks in this book are in the country, many on trails. Nevertheless, cities in Berkshire County, even the largest, are not far removed from landscape. In fact, the view from the top floor of the Crowne Plaza Hotel (corner of South and West Streets) rivals that of many ridges. Another kind of view exists, however: that of the manmade attributes of Berkshire. This book attempts to capture some of the history of the county at all sites while walking; here in Pittsfield it's appropriate to take a downtown tour. "Pittsfield: A Self-Guided Historic Walking Tour" is available for 25 cents at the Local History Room of the Berkshire Athenaeum, the modern building at the corner of Wendell and East Streets.

The Athenaeum itself, with its Local Authors Room, Children's Room, and Herman Melville Room, should be a stop on the tour. Start there and go next to the Berkshire Museum, on South Street just beyond Park Square. Founded in 1903 by the son of the founder of the Dalton paper mills, it offers art, history, and natural history. It runs a film and lecture series and other educational programs. Farther down South Street, the Colonial Theatre has reopened.

Here are some of the highlights of the rest of the tour. The self-guided tour map takes you past a series of buildings along Park Square, including the old Athenaeum, built in Venetian Gothic Revival style in 1876. It makes a statement, right? No longer a library, it now serves as the

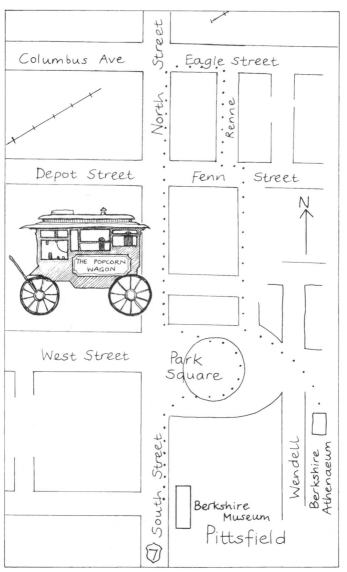

PITTSFIELD: DOWNTOWN

county district attorney's office and the midcounty registry of deeds, where you can purchase the official county road map, an invaluable tool for locating the out of the way, yet attractive enough to be framed.

In 1868 the then town of Pittsfield ended a 60-year struggle with Lenox about which was the appropriate town for the county seat by offering to build the Berkshire County Court House, next door. The state legislature then agreed to move the seat to the suitably gussied up building the town provided. Cross at Park Square, with its distinctive veterans' memorial, a map of Southeast Asia.

St. Stephen's Episcopal Church, directly across the square from Wendell Street, English Gothic in style, was built in 1889. The recently restored stained-glass windows include five by Tiffany and five by Tillinghast.

Across the street from St. Stephen's stands the elegant town hall, built in 1832. After years as a civic center, it is now inhabited by Berkshire Bank. Next, to the west, the First Church of Christ, Congregational, built in 1853, incorporates clock, bell, and boot scraper from a Charles Bulfinch–designed predecessor built in 1793. This substantial building serves as a reminder that from Colonial days right through to the mid-19th century, church and state were one in Massachusetts.

The Berkshire Bank, at the North Street corner, was built in 1894. In the warmer weather, it shares the site with its trademark, the popcorn wagon. The popper, now operated electrically, was once driven by steam. The wagon has stood on the corner since 1910 and is on the National Register of Historic Places. The Berkshire Corner, across North Street, was built in 1868 as the headquarters for Berkshire Life Insurance Company, now located in the imposing building across from the country club on South Street.

The Union Federal Savings Bank building, just north of the popcorn bank, was built in 1923 in a classical revival style. The Agricultural Bank building, farther down the same side of the street, looks just like a bank—a distinctly Greek one. The tour map notes that this is one of the few buildings on North Street that has all four sides exposed, while much of the street is a continuous wall of fronts.

The Rosa England block, just across Fenn Street, is one of Pittsfield's Victorian buildings. Although the facade has been adapted to the 20th century, most of the elegant features were preserved. Legacy Banks created Palace Park in 1994, site of the Palace Theater from 1913 to 1993. The flat-iron-shaped Eagle Building (1904) at the corner of Eagle Street is as efficient a use of available space next to the rail-road tracks as you could find. Although the newspaper itself has moved to larger quarters in a former mill, on South Church Street, the city is the richer for this distinctive structure and the sightly vest-pocket park that fills the tip of the triangle.

Across North Street is the new intermodal transportation center. At the corner with Union Street stands the New Barrington Stage home.

In a slight departure from the prescribed route, you might want to head east on Eagle Street and then south on Renne Street, to pass the home of the Berkshire Artisans and take a gander at the mural that decorates the wall. The First United Methodist Church at the corner of Fenn replaces a wooden structure that partially burned in 1871. The chancel window was created by Tiffany of New York.

The city government buildings are located to the south of Fenn Street. The city hall moved into the classic white Vermont marble building in 1967. It was built as a post office in 1910. The Central Fire Station, just beyond, on the National Register of Historic Places and another Berkshire Bank location, was built in 1895. The next year the city purchased horses to pull the heavy engines.

From here it is a short walk, continuing in the same direction, across East Street at the pedestrian crosswalk, to the Athenaeum.

CANOE MEADOWS

3 miles of trails available

This Massachusetts Audubon sanctuary consists of 262 acres of wetlands bordering the Housatonic River. Access is from Holmes Road just to the north of its junction with Pomeroy Avenue. (The Williams Street access is to the community gardens the sanctuary provides space for.) The property, with its 3 miles of trails, is open 9 AM to dusk, Tuesday through Sunday. The foliage filters the sound of traffic and the sight of nearby homes, so that even though the property is in a residential area, it carries you to the open fields of an earlier Pittsfield. There are no rest rooms, but outhouses are available.

Follow the maintenance road for starters; you might want to take the Wolf Pine Trail, as well. A blind to observe wildlife is located on a causeway. The essentially level trails across meadows and occasional bridges are skiable as long as wet areas are frozen under the snow. There is a self-guided nature tour. A donation is requested from nonmembers.

HIKE

BERRY POND

5 miles (2 hours hiking time)

Road approaches

From Park Square, Pittsfield, follow west on West Street, 2.5 miles; turn right on Churchill Street for 1.25 miles; and left at the chocolate-colored state forest sign on Cascade Street from which it is .5 mile to the state forest entrance. There is a small fee for parking, to use the bathing beach at Lulu Pond, or for camping.

From the north, turn right on Bull Hill Road, off Route 7 in Lanesborough, and go .5 mile; jog left and then right on

•

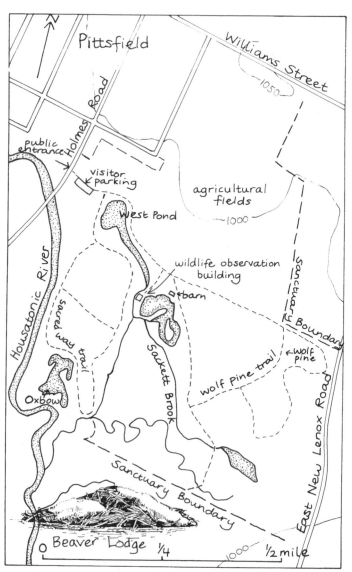

PITTSFIELD: CANOE MEADOWS

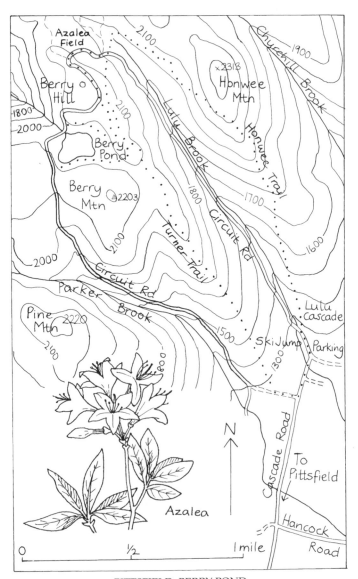

PITTSFIELD: BERRY POND

Balance Rock Road, which swings south for 1.3 miles to a Pittsfield State Forest gate. Drive in .5 mile to see an extraordinary balanced rock, on so delicate a base you would think any breeze would blow it over. The painted rock has been sandblasted to remove fools' names, which have reappeared. The rock is what is known as an erratic, carried in from the north by a glacier and deposited when the ice departed. Many trails lead to the part of the forest where you are headed, but consider Balance Rock a side trip; drive out the road and follow right to either Hancock Road or Dan Casey Drive; turn right and then left on Churchill to Cascade; right at the state forest sign.

Camping

Pittsfield State Forest has two campgrounds. The one at Parker Brook, to the west of the HQ, has 18 sites. The "comfort station," in state parlance, has flush toilets. The one at Berry Pond, your destination, has 13 sites, with pit toilets, meaning outhouses.

BERRY POND

This is a moderately steep hike, passing the common corner of the towns of Pittsfield, Lanesborough, and Hancock—where Berry Pond is actually located in Pittsfield State Forest. You pass through some extraordinary azalea fields, which bloom in early June; by a fine overlook into New York State; and to Berry Pond, elevation 2,060 feet, the highest natural body of water in Massachusetts. (The highest, at 3,200 feet, is on Mount Greylock, dug as water supply for Bascom Lodge.)

Because the blazing and signing of trails at Pittsfield has been erratic, you may wish to stop in at forest HQ to pick up the latest map or to inquire about the route. The problem is a bewildering excess of trails, some casually made by four-wheelers. From the state forest entrance it's .5 mile to Lulu Pond picnic area, where you park—and where you may want

to swim or at least wade at the end of the hike. Cross the
road from the parking lot. Take Honwee Trail, the second
below the gate, a woods road. It is blazed yellow, parallel to
and only a few feet above the Lulu Brook Trail and the Berry
Pond Circuit Road. It is pleasant to look down at the brook
itself as you pass through beech, maple, and birch forest,
with azaleas prominent on the understory or lower foliage.

Ignore the water supply road that comes in right in a few
minutes and continue on a moderately rising trail—a wet,
salamander heaven. It shows the marks of trail bikes in its
ruts. Ignore another trail from the right at 23 minutes. You
pass through a stand of pines. At a major intersection 15
minutes later, turn left across the brook and then up Berry
Pond Circuit Road. Although the traffic can be heavy on a
weekend during azalea season, the shoulders are walkable.
The three towns come together just south of the road at
about this point.

At 43 minutes on a sharp curve to the southeast, the
Taconic Skyline Trail, blazed white, exits the road, right. To
the left is your first chance to get on Turner Trail. Or, stay on
the road. You walk into the overlook at 52 minutes. The
mountains before you are the Catskills. Berry Pond, surrounded by tent sites, is 3 minutes ahead.

Backtrack to the Turner Trail, or follow trails on either
side of the pond (trails may be wet), or the Berkshire Hills
Ramble. Whichever way, you will end up on the Turner,
heading south-southeast. It is or has been blazed blue, but
not consistently. At first it passes along a plateau but eventually begins to descend steeply, crossed by trails at 10, 15,
and 36 minutes. This last you can take as a shortcut back to
the up-traffic side of the Circuit Road.

These are all well-used trails, so you may want to choose
weekdays, when the four-wheelers are less likely to be
prowling.

If you continue on Turner, at 40 minutes turn left on a
gravel road; then left again on Circuit Road after 5 minutes.
In four more minutes you will be back at the parking lot,
ready for a dip.

Many other combinations of trails are possible. The route described here is skiable, as are many of the other trails and unplowed roads. One special trail at Pittsfield State Forest is wheelchair accessible, the Tranquility Trail, west of the HQ building. (This trail is described in "Walks for the Blind and Disabled" below.)

HANCOCK

On the map, Hancock looks like what was left over maybe when the rest of Berkshire County was laid out: a long, narrow strip along the northwestern boundary of the county and thus the state, running from Williamstown to Richmond. It is impossible to drive from one end of Hancock to the other within the town lines. Six thousand acres of mountainous Pittsfield State Forest intervene. The three sections of the town of 721, north, village, and Shaker, draw mail from different post offices, draw wires from different utilities, and pledge different loyalties.

Settled in pre-Revolutionary times, the town was originally called Jericho, because the steep slopes were likened to the walls Joshua sent tumbling. When it was incorporated in 1776, it was named for the patriot whose large signature decorates the Declaration of Independence, John Hancock. Samuel Hand, who represented the town in the state government in the 1790s, asked his fellow lawmakers for hazardous duty pay—or at least a clothing allowance—because "the mountains are so steep that one can not climb out without spoiling the knees of his pantaloons, or go back without spoiling his seat."

The biggest business by far is Jiminy Peak, once solely a ski area and now a mountain resort. The second largest business is the not-for-profit Hancock Shaker Village. Second-home developments are rising. A few farms, a few stores, some bed and breakfasts and restaurants, as well as the more commercial area along Route 20 out of Pittsfield, make up the rest of town.

HIKE

SHAKER MOUNTAIN

6.5 miles (3 hours hiking time)

Road approaches

From Park Square in Pittsfield follow Route 20 west for 5 miles. Park in the lot for Hancock Shaker Village, on your left across the Hancock town line.

Most people taking this hike will want to tour Hancock Shaker Village first, to learn about the souls who built the industrial and holy sites you are about to visit. The Shaker religion reached its zenith in this country in the 1830s. These celibates believed that all work was an expression of God's glory; thus their furniture and craftsmanship are both simple and exquisite. A tour of 20 restored buildings, including crafts workshops and the famous round barn, takes at least two hours. There is a fee. The village is open May through October, 9:30 AM to 5 PM. The Visitors' Center, adjacent to the parking lot, contains rest rooms, lunch shop, information center, and museum shop. Picnic tables are available. The nearest camping is at Pittsfield State Forest.

SHAKER MOUNTAIN

> *'Tis the gift to be simple,*
> *'Tis the gift to be free,*
> *'Tis the gift to come down*
> *Where we ought to be. . . .*
> —Shaker hymn

The first simple gift you will receive from the Shakers, or at least the nonprofit corporation that runs their village, is the hospitality of the visitors' center. You will pay a reduced fee for parking—unless you decide to tour the village as well. (Then the full fee applies.) The first part of the hike is on village property; the rest is in Pittsfield State Forest. This remarkable hike takes you past the unrestored remains of the North Family or industrial grouping of Hancock Shakers. Included are the village's water system, mill sites, dams, the foundations of a residence, 150-year-old cart roads, charcoal-burning sites, stone walls, and hilltop holy sites of both the Hancock village and the New Lebanon (New York) Shaker Village. After that, with any luck at all, you will come down where you ought to be, right where you started.

Use the crosswalk to get to the north side of Route 20 and to the fields behind the 1793 Meeting House, the most westerly of the village buildings. Head north to the logging road. The trail departs north from a cleared log landing two minutes from the highway. Laid out by the Boy Scouts, it is marked by green triangles with white circles. Even if these have not been kept up, you begin on an unmistakable cart road that soon follows the western side of Shaker Brook. The stone walls may have been laid up in 1845. Eight minutes from the highway you arrive at the lower dam, the beginning of a sophisticated water system. The pipe fills a reservoir from which it traveled underground to the village where it first powered machinery, then supplied the wash rooms (the Shaker laundry), then the stables, then the mills, and then the fields to water the cattle. The old bridge above the dam has been replaced. Cross the brook.

As you follow down the eastern side of the stream you pass first an industrial site with a pit for a water wheel and then the cellar hole for the North Family residence. To imagine its size, compare with the Brick Dwelling in the village, although this one was made of wood. At 15 minutes into the walk, not counting the time you have taken to examine the ruins, turn left up the hill, through second-growth hardwood with some shagbark hickory and hemlock, on what was probably the Shakers' original cart road to their holy site.

At 27 minutes bear left where a branch of the road continues straight. This was a charcoal-burning site. At 34 minutes cross under power lines that serve airplane beacon

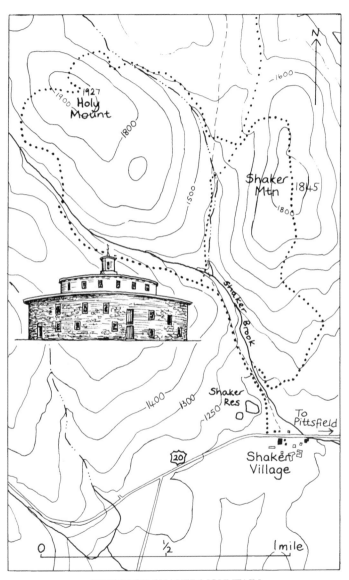

1927
Holy
Mount
1900
1800

1600

Shaker
Mtn 1845

1800

1500

Shaker Brook

1400 1300 1250

Shaker
Res

To
Pittsfield

20

Shaker
Village

0   ½   1 mile

N

HANCOCK: SHAKER MOUNTAIN

lights for the Pittsfield airport. You switch back to cross under the lines again.

At 44 minutes you enter the overgrown field that was the Hancock Shakers' holy ground, which they called Mount Sinai, now referred to as Shaker Mountain. The Shakers did not permit nonbelievers on this site. In 1841 or 1842, all Shaker communities were required to clear the summit of a nearby hill, focusing on a "fountain" or hexagonal fence surrounding a marble slab, about which they marched, sang, and danced in May and September. A depression in the blackberry bushes beside the trail marks the fountain; little else remains at Mount Sinai. More artifacts are visible at Holy Mount, about a mile as the bird flies across the valley. Shakers called to each other across the chasm.

The trail follows along the ridge and then turns left, into the valley. At about 50 minutes, it switches back through a lovely hemlock grove. At 1:03 you come out on a lumber road. Turn left. If you wish a hike of one hour and 30 minutes, follow straight back to the village. Otherwise turn right almost immediately. This road follows to the left of a stone wall. At the end of the wall (1:18), bear left down the hill. The trail swings right, between sections of another stone wall and across a brook (1:23). The forest in this section has not been lumbered as ruthlessly as has the forest in the valley and on Shaker Mountain. Follow up the hill to a junction of walls and trails (1:27), where you turn left, again following a stone wall.

At 1:36 pass an opening in the wall that probably admitted a cart road from the New Lebanon community to its holy ground. At 1:41 you arrive at what was a gated entrance, elevation 1,927 feet (higher than Mount Sinai). Follow the wall, on the inside, left to the feast ground and the foundations of the shelter (1:44). Although the Shakers planted a row of pines around each site, the CCC planted the pine trees inside, in the 1930s. If you head into the woods directly in front of the shelter, you may find the depression in the ground that marks the fountain site. There was an altar 10 yards west of the fountain.

Downhill from the altar is a beautiful specimen of the wall-maker's art, 3 feet at the base and tapering to the top, 18 feet long. The brethren must have taken 350 man-days to build the wall around the sacred lot, not to mention the other walls you have seen.

Starting in front of the shelter, head west, bearing right downhill on a trail that reaches an opening in the wall (1:53). Although the path generally follows the wall to the left, it swings out in an arc before rejoining at the corner. This section of trail, which is not based on an old road and has not experienced much wear, is hard to follow even with the markers. The corner of the wall encloses a natural amphitheater (2:03), containing a spring. If you did not stop to picnic at either summit, this would be a good spot. Cross the brook below the corner and follow steeply up the hill, along the path, until it comes out on a fire road (2:20). Turn left. The brook is on your right. You pass the first of several wide spots on the road, which were charcoal-burning sites. You may find some pieces of charcoal. Follow the fire road until it turns left, uphill, while you continue straight on the older cart road to a brook crossing (2:29). From here follow the green triangles down the branch of the brook to take in a Shaker marble quarry.

At 2:41 you return to the main cart road (bear right) at the site of the high dam, which is largely washed out. It may have been constructed in 1810. Just below, the Shakers built a sawmill that bridged the stream. Logs were loaded at the retaining wall on the far side. The depressions on the near side were mill foundations. This mill, which ran on water power or steam when water wasn't sufficient, was built mid-19th century and burned in 1926.

Follow the cart road to the log landing. Total round trip is just about 3 hours, counting only travel time. It would be possible to ski Shaker Mountain but not Holy Mount. A ski loop, the same as for an abbreviated hike, would return via the lumber road you meet after descending Shaker Mountain.

DALTON

A town of about 6,892 population at a junction of Routes 8 and 9, east of Pittsfield, Dalton has been dominated by paper manufacturing virtually since its incorporation in 1784. It is still a paper town. In 1799 Henry Wiswell, John Willard, and Zenas Crane began a mill on the Housatonic that produced the first paper made in Berkshire County. The history of the forerunners of Crane & Company is one of rapid technological progress and spectacular fires. Local residents attributed the success of the company in part to the quality of a spring on the premises. Early on, the company made collars, bond, bank notes, and parchment; now it is best known for manufacturing the paper on which the U.S. currency is printed. The Crane Paper Museum on Route 9, west of town, portrays the history of papermaking; additional artifacts are exhibited at the Berkshire Museum in Pittsfield.

Because the AT passes through town, Dalton is well known to through-hikers as a pleasant and friendly stop, with an array of places to eat and stay along the main street. The AT passes by the Boulders, a rocky and wooded parcel that nudges the heart of town.

Wahconah Brook falls near the Windsor border. It was known to Indians but "discovered" by William Cleveland while he was looking for a beehive. He built a dam above the falls and a flume around them to drop the water on the overshot wheel of a grist mill, about 1770. His millstones were fashioned in France and hauled to the site by boat to Boston and oxen across the Bay Colony. About 1800 Jacob Booth added a sawmill to the site.

As is true of other county falls and cliffs, Wahconah Falls comes with an assortment of Indian traditions. In one story, Wahconah, daughter of a prominent chief, was denied a suitor from an enemy tribe, so she jumped into the brook. In another, Wahconah said she would marry the brave who could leap across the chasm above the falls, which was narrower in those days. Of the two who made the attempts the

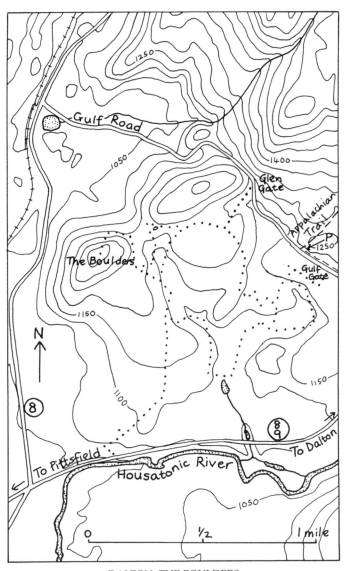

DALTON: THE BOULDERS

wrong one cleared and the right one landed in the brook. So she jumped in after him and they went over the falls together to their deaths.

WALKS

THE BOULDERS

Various trails leading to the Boulders themselves, about 4 miles (2 hours)

Crane & Co., headquarters in Dalton, opened the site of a former family lodge to the public in 1994. It is a wonderful piece of wooded land surrounded by urban sections of Dalton, Pittsfield, and Lanesborough. Added to the fun of investigating the property is a fine view of the surrounding countryside from the eponymous boulders at nearly 1,375 feet.

Although a path leaves directly across from Crane & Co. Government Gate on Route 9, you get more of a feel for the property by parking at either the Gulf Gate or a corner of the Appalachian Trail, both at the Dalton end of Gulf Road. From Route 8, turn east (summer only) between Pasta's Arizona Pizza Company and Hut's Pub & Grill. From Dalton, take Park Street past the DPW garage. (Warning: watch out for people driving too fast on this narrow, twisty, gravel road.)

From either entrance you will soon make your way to the main woods road, formerly driveway to the estate. Trails are blazed different colors on blocks of wood, which may help you keep track of the route back. As you begin to climb, your hear industrial noises, perhaps from Unistress. An initial lookout, shortly before turning south to the summit, is a short scramble off the road. The drive/road ends at the circle just before the major lookout, which reveals a surprisingly bucolic view of Pittsfield. People have been unable to resist applying graffiti to the boulders, serving to remind the visitor that it is only a few hundred yards to downtown.

The Boulders

WAHCONAH FALLS

A few hundred feet

The popular waterfall and gorge is located at Wahconah Falls State Park on Route 9 in Dalton. Coming from Dalton center, turn right at the sign, passing Dalton Tractor. About 1 mile up gravel Wahconah Road lies the parking lot. There is no fee, no camping, and no lifeguard, but there is a composting toilet. A sometime party spot, at last visit it had accumulated a good deal of trash. (It is hard to understand why the public can't treat a beautiful resource with respect.) On this 53-acre tract you will find a deep gulf, rocky ledges, large hemlocks, and a scattering of picnic grills. Trails meander through the woods on either side of the brook. The falls dive deeply over ledges below Windsor Reservoir on a tributary of the Housatonic. Deep pools below beckon the visitor who wants to cool off—strictly at your own risk, of course. (For a map, see the Dalton/Windsor map under "Windsor Jambs.")

Wahconah Falls

WINDSOR

Once Plantation No. 4, the land making up Windsor was sold to a consortium of buyers in 1762, prototypes of today's land developers: buy a chunk of wilderness, survey it, and try to sell the lots for a good profit. The boundaries weren't exactly the same, including part of present-day Dalton and Cheshire but not the present northern part of Windsor— which was considered a section of plantation No. 5, Cummington (in Hampshire County).

As sometimes happens to developers even now, the lots moved slowly, which made it hard for the consortium to pay off its notes; furthermore, many of those who bought were also speculators rather than pioneers, so time passed before any significant settlement. Still, in 1771, residents petitioned to incorporate as Gageborough, after the pre-Revolutionary governor of the colony. In 1777 they petitioned to change the name, British general Gage having fallen out of favor in 1775. By the end of that century, the area was a thriving farming community, with the usual accumulation of mills. When the sons and daughters of farmers went west and when the railroad failed to pass through town, Windsor became a byway.

By the beginning of the 20th century, General Alfred E. Bates had begun accumulating former farms in the north of town, while Helen Gamwell Ely was accumulating land to the south to form her Helenscourt. In the 1920s, Elizabeth C. T. Miller bought the Bates estate. Mrs. Ely remarried Lieutenant Colonel Arthur D. Budd, who also acquired the Miller property. Thus, the 3,000 acres of Notchview Reservation, nearly a quarter of the town, resulted from the union of two large estates, located on Route 9. Now owned by TTOR, Notchview borders 1,616 acres of Windsor State Forest and is nearby a similar-sized tract that is part of the state forest and part of a Wildlife Management Area, presumably fixing the character of the town for some time to come.

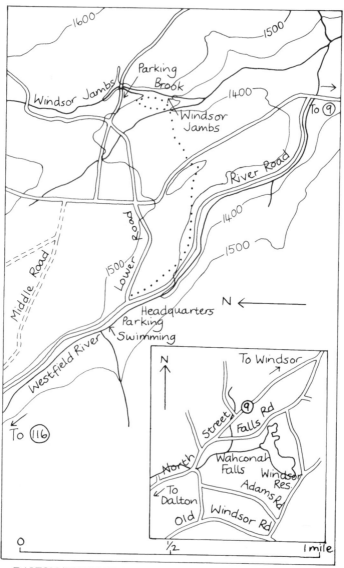

DALTON/WINDSOR: WAHCONAH FALLS/WINDSOR JAMBS

Camping

Camping is available for a small fee in season at Windsor Jambs State Park, part of the state forest. The area is just east and north of Notchview, on River Road (signs on Route 116 and Route 9 direct you to the park). A foot trail along Steep Bank Brook connects the Jambs with Notchview, about 3 miles to the Budd Visitors' Center. At the campground, a stream is dammed for swimming. Tourist accommodations are not available in Windsor.

WALK

WINDSOR JAMBS

3 miles (1.5 hours)

When people talk about the Jambs, they mean the state park with its swimming area (follow the signs from Routes 116 or 9). Strictly speaking, however, the Jambs is, or are, a nearby gorge, the name derived perhaps from the stream's narrowed route through a rock doorway. Park in the lot by park HQ. Across the road, generally bear right through the camping area for the Jambs Trail, which actually begins by the solar toilets. You can also drive to the scenic gorge on the gravel Lower Road, but to do so would be to miss out on a 3-mile, round-trip stroll through a deep evergreen forest. The leisurely path, blazed blue, wanders in its own insouciant way through spruce, hemlock, and even some pine and fir. The trail is wet and, as it runs beside the Jambs, requires sure-footedness, so wear hiking shoes. For the best effect, at the junction follow the trail to the lower Jambs, then work up along the edge, protected by the fence, to upper Jambs. The trail back leaves from the parking lot. Jambs Brook has cut deeply into slabs of rock, tumbling over many small falls, a pleasing sight even when, in mid-summer, not much water passes through.

HIKE

NOTCHVIEW/JUDGE'S HILL

5.5 miles (2.25 hours hiking time)

Road approaches

Take Route 9 east from Pittsfield, through Dalton, where 8A joins, and up the long hill to Windsor. The entrance to Notchview is 1 mile east of the junction where Route 8A departs north. That road drops south from Route 116 out of Adams, an alternate course for people setting sail for Notchview from North County.

JUDGE'S HILL

The Arthur D. Budd Visitors' Center, at the parking lot, serves as an information booth and provides a place for

Trail heads, Notchview

cross-country skiers to wax and warm. Rest rooms are available. There are picnic tables and there is a water source, but no camping is allowed.

TTOR maintains this 3,108-acre reservation, which takes its name from the view from Lt. Col. Budd's former home through a notch eastward into the hills of Cummington. Route 9 passes through the Notch. Budd, a World War II hero, donated the property in 1965. The Trustees charge a nominal fee to nonmembers for use. The property shows traces of farming the soil of these hills, known as "rock farming," and of the later era of gentlemen's estates.

The 25 miles of trails on the property pass through trees that have grown up on former fields—and also some fields that are cut. Although you only climb 297 feet to the summit of Judge's Hill, the highest land in Windsor, you start at an elevation of 2,000 feet. This quality of highland plateau, complete with evergreen forests, harsh climate, rocky soil, bogs, and deep stream crevasses, distinguishes Notchview. Wildlife here includes white-tailed deer, bobcat, nesting hawks, and the occasional bear.

You may choose any combination of a multitude of well-marked and well-maintained trails. As a 5.5-miler, for instance, for a morning's hike (or ski), walk straight ahead from the parking area, leaving the barn on the left, and turning left on the Circuit Trail. You walk gently up through a wet spruce area. At 12 minutes, turn left on Judge's Hill Trail. (As well as blazes, ample signs let you know which trail you're on.) At first you lose elevation, crossing Shaw Road (gravel) and descending through mixed hardwoods and across a bridge. Then you begin to climb moderately, through an area marked by large glacial boulders.

After 31 minutes you achieve the summit, marked by the stone remains of the fireplace of the Judge's "fort," laid up without mortar. Most of the surrounding growth is quite young; the Judge must have had a marvelous view when the land was cleared. Judge James M. Barker was the most prominent member of a social and sporting group known as the Windsor Club, which held weekend hunting and fishing

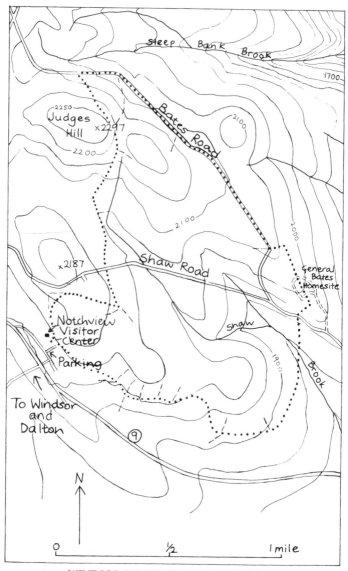

WINDSOR: NOTCHVIEW/JUDGE'S HILL

trips on the property. He erected the stone lunch stop, walled around and complete with stone tables and benches, about the turn of the century.

It takes 9 minutes to descend to Bates Road, a gravel surface on which you turn right. You pass between the cellar holes and stone walls of some of the two dozen families who at one time lived in the area. In one, a rabbit warren has been cleverly burrowed under a concrete slab. Is this the site of the Babbitt Axe Factory? Could these be the Babbitt rabbits? The Steep Bank Brook Trail, which departs left, would take you to Windsor Jambs.

Pick up the Bumpus Trail, left, through open fields past a shelter to the Gen. Bates home site. He fought Indians in Kansas and Wyoming. His cousin, Herman, was famous for the quality of the butter he produced on this highland farm, becoming known as Butter Bates. The open fields provide a nice contrast to traveling the woods. The Bumpus Trail turns abruptly right, crossing Shaw Road (1:14) and descending steeply into a gorge. It crosses a bridge over Shaw Brook, then climbs through evergreens. Continue straight at the Y, 9 minutes later. Follow the signs toward the Visitors' Center, coming out on the open Sawmill Field, crossing it, and picking up the Circuit Trail back to the parking lot (1:55).

Among the many alternatives for walks as well as hikes is the mile-long, self-guided interpretive trail in the Hume Brook area across Route 9 at Notchview that explains the principles of forest land management, with an emphasis on forest aesthetics and wildlife. TTOR issues separate maps for hiking and skiing; a large map is posted by the parking lot. Bring a picnic; spend the day.

NORTH COUNTY

NORTH COUNTY

CHESHIRE

Cheshire in early days was called New Providence by homesick Rhode Islanders. Colonel Joab Stafford led a group of his townspeople to the Battle of Bennington on August 15, 1777. A monument and a Wildlife Management Area honor him. In 1801 the town combined all its milk production for one day into a 1,255-pound cheese, which oxen dragged to a boat on the Hudson River and thence to Washington to honor newly elected president Thomas Jefferson. Most of the Cheshire lakes, the headwaters of the Hoosic River, falling within the town borders, were dammed to provide a head at low water for the former Adams Print Works. The AT crosses the river and Route 8 in town on its way to climb into the Mount Greylock State Reservation via Outlook Avenue. Many through-hikers on the trail stop in Cheshire to pick up mail forwarded to them c/o General Delivery at the post office and to sleep at a friendly church.

WALK

ASHUWILLTICOOK TRAIL

3.2 miles (1.25 hours); the trail currently extends 11 miles

You need no longer worry about trains along this section of roadbed, although in the mid-19th century the Hoosic River Railroad connected major east-west lines in Pittsfield and North Adams. Now it is a wonderful water-level route, re-created into a popular, paved biking, rollerblading, baby stroller, and walking trail, which so far joins the Berkshire Mall, on the Pittsfield line, with a visitors' center in downtown Adams. Hopes have been kindled to run it through North Adams and Williamstown, with a spur to Clarksburg.

Pedestrian/bicycle bridge over Hoosic River, Ashuwillticock Trail

You can walk any section you like, or the whole thing. The portion along Cheshire Reservoir (Hoosac Lake) is probably the most scenic and the portion through the "Jungle" is of most wildlife interest. So here's a bit of each for two cars. Leave auto No. 1 at Cheshire Harbor (turn off Route 8 to the east near the bottom of the hill between Berkshire Outfitters and the State Police barracks). Parking is along the road, staying out of the way of homeowners. Drive the second car south to Farnam's Crossing, a road running west from Route 8 that crosses the reservoir on a causeway. (Here is a universally accessible bathroom.) After parking, walk north, looking out at the Greylock massif over the water. Just before you reach the road you will pass the dam that controls the water level. The Hoosic River was dammed in the 19th century to provide a backup supply for water power for a downstream mill. Take care crossing

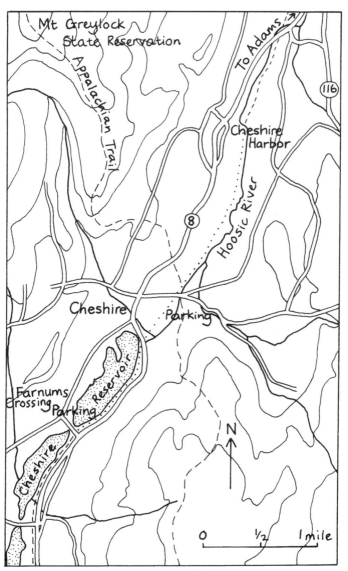

CHESHIRE: ASHUWILLTICOOK TRAIL

Route 8 at the blinking light. Follow the trail behind the restaurant. Cross the bridge over Kitchen Brook. You pass by some backyards with barking dogs. Play the part of the train as you cross Church Street (and the Appalachian Trail). Soon you are removed from houses and dogs, as South Brook enters from the southeast. Stafford Hill rises northeast and the Greylock massif, northwest.

Natives call this section the Jungle, as the 10-foot-wide Hoosic writhes through swampland. Alligators you need not worry about; however, nesting snapping turtles can be a problem in late spring. The calcareous (lime-based) wetlands west of the tracks, and marshes and shrub swamps east of the tracks, are fine habitat for a variety of water creatures. Wood-duck platforms dot the wetlands, deer and muskrat tracks follow the stream. You may see snowshoe hare, pheasant, occasional fox, and some naturally reproducing brown trout as well as stocked trout. Note that although heading north, you are going downstream. Route 8 is close at hand, but not noticeable except for the distant sound of a truck downshifting. You see a gouged hillside of gravel pits to the left.

A brick building belonging to the town of Adams introduces the first road for 3 miles. This is the pumping station for two artesian wells. Around the corner appears a bridge. Welcome to Cheshire Harbor, said to be named because it harbored runaway slaves, a lovely spot with an old swimming hole, somewhat silted in. Now the river is on the left, with Route 8 just the far side. Car No. 1 awaits.

Of course the Ashuwillticook is designed for biking, especially family outings, given its flat, paved surface. Since the local Berkshire "B-buses" have bike racks on the front, you could pedal between the Berkshire Mall to Adams and bus back. The trail is open to cross-country skiing in the winter.

ADAMS AND MOUNT GREYLOCK

Adams, first East Township, then East Hoosuck, was named for Revolutionary War hero Samuel Adams in 1778.

View of Adams from Mount Greylock

Its remarkable ethnic heritage began with English Quakers, whose vitality carved an industrial center from the wilderness, and continued through successive waves of immigrants who came to labor in those industries: Irish, Scots, Germans, French Canadians, and Poles. Although the textile mills have ceased and although its northern end was lopped off to form North Adams, Adams remains a bustling town of 8,809, with all the accommodations and services a walker could want, including a visitors' center. Most stores and restaurants are along Route 8, which goes by different names such as Columbia and Park Streets. The statue of President William McKinley in front of the library honors a friend of a foremost Adams family, the Plunketts. McKinley's high tariff policies benefited the local cloth manufacturers (cf. "Protection Avenue" in North Adams).

Although the summit of Mount Greylock lies in the town of Adams, the Mount Greylock State Reservation encompasses 12,500 acres of hilly land in the towns of Adams, Cheshire, Lanesborough, New Ashford, North Adams, and Williamstown. But you only have to look up in Adams to understand why the town feels a special regard for the mountain that looms over it. Mount Greylock is a close, intimate friend.

Greylock is the tallest peak in southern New England at 3,491 feet. It is surrounded by half a dozen lower eminences, most of which are still higher than anything else in Massachusetts, Connecticut, and Rhode Island: Saddleball (3,238), Mount Fitch (3,110), Mount Williams (2,951), Mount Prospect (2,690), Stony Ledge (2,580), and Ragged Mountain (2,451).

So it is not as high as most of the Catskills, Adirondacks, White Mountains, or the Green Mountains even—all of which you can see from Greylock. At one time the Appalachians, of which Greylock is a part, stood Himalayan high, six times their present altitude, but time and weather have eroded them.

In the early 19th century, before the more spectacular, western scenery in this country was accessible, Greylock created a lot of excitement. All the great American writers and naturalists, such as Thoreau, Hawthorne, and Melville, made their pilgrimages to Greylock. The first person to publish an account of his visit, in 1799, was the president of Yale, Timothy Dwight, who said "the view was immense and of amazing grandeur. . . ." It inspired prose, poetry, fiction, and energetic enjoyment of the out-of-doors.

Not surprisingly, given the popular destination it has been and still is, the summit is reached by paved roads from North Adams (Notch Road) and from Lanesborough (Rockwell Road), which meet a mile from the top, from whence they travel together as Summit Road. A gravel-surfaced road, known as New Ashford or Greylock, climbs from the west to Rockwell Road not far below a gravel spur known as Sperry Road. Formerly a way to the public campgrounds, they are now accessible by a mile's hike from parking on Rockwell Road. Tent sites are distributed discreetly in a spruce grove. Stony Ledge, at the end of Sperry Road, provides a spectacular view of the Hopper, a V-shaped wedge worn by erosion on the western side.

The summit has limited development, such as broadcast

towers and communications dishes. A 100-foot-high War
Memorial Tower, a design clearly influenced by lighthouses
along the seashore, 130 miles away, was erected on Greylock
in the 1930s to honor the dead of World War I. The state-
owned Bascom Lodge, built by the state and CCC during
the New Deal, provides modest accommodations and good,
hearty food, in season (reservations required). Enthusiastic
state interpreters lead walks and conduct programs to
explain the natural and human history of the mountain,
departing the lodge, the campground, and Greylock Glen
(in Adams).

A 7.8-mile segment of the 2,050-mile-long AT transects
the reservation from south to north, a ribbon that hangs
over most of the peaks. Remember: the AT is blazed white.
Of the five 3-sided shelters on the reservation, two are associated with the AT. Ten side trails to the AT, blazed blue,
together with 11 other trails and the AT, total 43 miles of
hiking in the Greylock range—routes shorter or longer,
steeper or more gentle, fit just about every walker's time
and ambition.

The War Memorial Tower, open during posted hours,
extends the view from the summit to 70 or 100 miles in clear
conditions. Innumerable more local views reveal Adams
from the east of the summit, the farms of Williamstown
from the trail intersection on Mount Prospect, the peak itself
from Ragged Mountain, the lakes and rounded hills of mid-
Berkshire from Jones's Nose or Rounds' Rock.

Views on the mountains include tumbling streams.
March Cataract flows best when the snows melt. You can
see it from Route 7 in front of Mount Greylock Regional
High School. A trail from the campground leads to it. The Deer
Hill Trail from the campground passes a falls on Roaring
Brook. Money Brook Falls, also tucked into the Hopper, can
be reached by a side trail to the Money Brook Trail.

Most of the vegetation on lower Greylock is northern
hardwood: beech, birch, maple, and few evergreens. In the
southern portions of the reservation, recent second growth
fills formerly farmed fields. Here and there on the mountain's

East side of Mt. Greylock

steep slopes stand aged trees, in areas not cut for railroads
or other development over the years. In particular the 1,600
acres of the Hopper, on the west side, contain red spruce
stands nearly 200 years old. The state has designated the
Hopper a Natural Area. The federal government, together
with the Society of American Foresters, has recognized
these spruces as a National Natural Landmark. To protect
the Hopper, it is a low-impact area, excluding vehicles,
campfires, and camping, but available for study and hiking.
    Greylock's upper reaches are covered by a boreal type of
spruce, balsam fir, and yellow birch forest, probably the

only example of such woods in Massachusetts. The bogs and stunted fir growth near the summits of Greylock and Saddleback are similar to the vegetation on the Canadian Shield—the forest of the far north. Your experience as a hiker arriving in them is exhilarating.

The variety of wildlife matches the diverse vegetation. Forty state-listed rare or endangered species have been seen on the reservation, as well as birds as unusual as Swainson's thrush and the blackpoll warbler. Viewers come to watch a variety of hawks (and hang gliders) performing their aerobatics by taking advantage of updrafts on the steepest part of the east face. Common wildlife include the white-tailed deer, bobcat, snowshoe hare, cottontail rabbit, ruffed grouse, woodcock, raccoon, red squirrel, chipmunk, fox, skunk, woodchuck, and the porcupine that hang around the shelters to chew your hiking boots if you leave them unattended. Bear, the eastern coyote, wild turkey, fisher, and raven have recently returned to the reservation, as surrounding farm fields grow over.

Berkshire County is blessed by 150,000 acres of land protected from development, approximately one-quarter its total area. The Greylock Reservation stands as the flagship of the state's park system and as the jewel of the county's public and private holdings.

This book describes walks and hikes in the summit area and in the campground area. The walks are the one from Notch Road in to the ridge of Prospect Mountain, the Overlook Trail, Stony Ledge, March Cataract, Deer Hill, and Rounds' Rock. It describes four hikes: Cheshire Harbor Trail, from the southwest; Bellows Pipe Trail from the north; Hopper Trail from the west; and Stony Ledge/Roaring Brook from the southeast. Dogs are allowed only on leash at the campground.

WALKS

ADAMS

ROLLAND G. DUVAL NATURE TRAIL

HOOSAC VALLEY HIGH SCHOOL

1.3 miles (35 minutes)

Most of this pleasant, rolling trail is in Cheshire, as is the high school, but it begins near the main gate, 2 miles south of downtown on Route 116 in Adams. The sign is to the left as you enter; the best place to park is the school's north lot, from which you can simply walk down the hill to the trail. Of the numerous connected loops, stay on the gravel. It will take you on the hillside around the school. At one time the trail appears to have been blazed. Signs with nature notes remain.

The initial portion is over bog bridges through a marshy area. As the trail begins to bear away from the school, at eight minutes follow the left leg of the Y, uphill. You are on a second-growth pine hillside, no doubt formerly grazing land. Playing fields appear on your right, with some views of the Greylock Range. Take a left again behind the playing fields. Soon you see farm fields on the left, where someone has thoughtfully placed a bench. At 22 minutes you cross a bridge and two minutes later another bridge over the same brook. You end up behind the football field, from which you can make your way to your car.

GREYLOCK

OVERLOOK TRAIL

2.5 miles (1 hour)

Try the Overlook Trail from the summit, fairly rigorous going that passes by fine overlooks into the Hopper. Depart from the television tower, except turn right instead of following the Hopper Trail. Descent is constant through mixed woods to Notch Road. Cross it into the woods again at about 10 minutes, continuously losing altitude until the stream crossing just above March Cataract (40 minutes). Don't overlook the overlooks, which are down short, unmarked trails in this vicinity. Shortly you come out on the Hopper Trail, at which you turn left to climb back up to the TV tower.

CAMPGROUND TRAILS

Stony Ledge, 2 miles; March Cataract, about 2 miles; Deer Hill, 2.25 miles

Several trails depart from the campground, including a self-guided nature and cultural walk. Consult the supervisor at the contact station for detailed information on their present state. The most spectacular is simply to continue up gravel Sperry Road 1 mile from the contact station to Stony Ledge, with its breathtaking view over the sheer depths of the Hopper to Greylock and Fitch. The road rises but this is an easy walk on an open road, suitable even for sneakers. It is also possible to drive on Sperry Road on Sunday afternoons. The afternoon is the best time to make the trip, because the sun strikes on the far ledges. An intriguing alternative from the same perch, however, is watching the sun rise over the highest peak in Massachusetts.

Other walks include a good bit of up-and-down, and so require stout shoes. A short but rugged trail departs across from the contact station, up a former road and then right, up and along a sidehill, then steeply down, less than 1 mile in total, to the foot of March Cataract. Although a good flow of water tumbles down at all seasons, the walk is especially recommended in high water, when you will be well wetted before you stand on the midstream rocks—if you can— gazing up the gleaming wet stone face. It is dangerous to make this trip in the winter, because the trail can be icy and cuts uncertainly along the sidehill, but it is a thrill to hear the water plunging beneath the ice. Note: this trail is less worn than most in the reservation and therefore harder to follow.

Departing Sperry Road on the same side as the contact station but a few hundred feet farther in, the Deer Hill Trail follows Roaring Brook, sharing the Roaring Brook Trail at first but turning left after 200 yards, passing Deer Hill Falls (1 mile) and what may be the oldest, untouched stand of trees (hemlock) on the reservation, and starting fairly steeply up, past a lean-to, and coming out on the carriage road. Turn left to arrive at Sperry Road and left again to return to the contact station (2.25 miles). If you don't turn on Sperry Road, you will come out on the Hopper Trail above the campground.

MOUNT PROSPECT FROM NOTCH ROAD

1 mile (30 minutes)

Climbing from the valley to the peak of Prospect is the steepest hike around (it begins partway along the Money Brook Trail, which in turn begins at the same point as the Hopper Trail). It is possible to get the same view, however, by driving up Notch Road 3 miles from the gate to the AT crossing at the stand of tall spruce trees. There is an obvious parking area beyond and a big sign. Follow the white blazes down and then up. Where the AT meets the Prospect Trail, on the ridge (.5 mile), an opening gives a fine view of Williamstown and especially the Galusha Farm, with cleared fields below you.

ROUNDS' ROCK

1.25 miles (35 minutes)

About 3 miles north of the Visitors' Center on Rockwell Road you will find a two- or three-car pull-off on the right.

Walk a couple hundred feet farther on the road to a rock outcropping, left, and the beginning of the Rounds' Rock Trail. Jabez Rounds farmed this area in the early 19th century. You walk up a wooded hill to an open field covered with blueberry bushes. In berry season the main trail gets lost as people explore productive side paths; but continue straight, into the woods, by a town bound (N.A. stands for New Ashford). Once again pass into an open, stony field with berries. Two trails lead to magnificent overlooks, the first south; the second southwest. The next stop is the remains of a plane, which crashed in 1945 while delivering the *New York Times* to Berkshire County. At this point, the Rounds' Rock Trail connects to the Northrup Trail, which will eventually join to the Visitors' Center. If you stay on Rounds' Rock, you will return to the trail on which you began, near the road.

HIKES

CHESHIRE HARBOR TRAIL

6.6 miles (2.5 hours hiking time)

Road approaches

At the statue of former president McKinley in front of the library in Adams turn west off Route 8 onto Maple Street. At .4 mile turn left on West Road; .5 mile later, right on West Mountain Road at the sign for Mount Greylock Greenhouses. The road ends at a turnaround, the site of a former farmhouse, after 1.6 miles. Most of the land is part of Greylock Glen, state-owned with an uncertain future, but the trailhead will remain open.

Camping

Peck's Brook shelter, a three-sided Adirondack lean-to, is attained by a separate 1-mile trail that departs from the

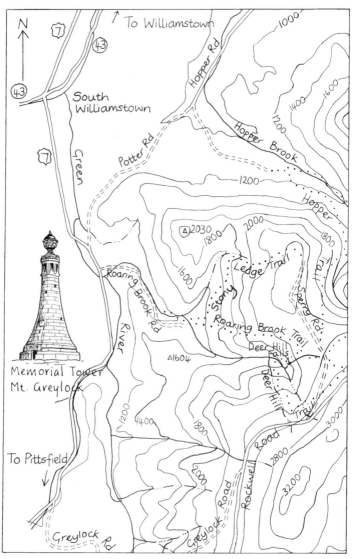

N

To Williamstown

7
43

43

South
Williamstown

7

Green

Hopper Rd

Potter Rd

Hopper Brook

1000

1400

1600

1200

1200

Hopper

△2030

1800

2000

1800

Ledge Trail

Stony

Sperry Rd

Roaring Brook Rd

River

Roaring Brook Trail

Deer Hills

1600

△1604

Memorial Tower
Mt. Greylock

Deer Hill

Trail

3000

To Pittsfield

1200

1400

1800

2000

Rockwell Road

2800

3200

Greylock Road

Greylock Rd

ADAMS: MOUNT GREYLOCK

ADAMS: MOUNT GREYLOCK

junction of Rockwell, Notch, and Summit Roads. Bascom Lodge, at the summit, has limited accommodations (reservations required) as well as food. All summit buildings are closed from late October until Memorial Day, but some protection may be found at the Thunderbolt Ski Shelter, with fireplace (BYOM—bring your own matches!) on the AT just below the summit parking lot, to the north of the War Memorial Tower.

CHESHIRE HARBOR TRAIL

Mount Greylock is very close to its east side approaches, although the summit is more of a haul than it looks as you stand on the old field at the end of the open section of West Mountain Road. Cheshire Harbor Trail is the shortest and easiest of the hiking routes to the summit, not only because of its directness but because it begins at a good elevation. It rises from 1,800 feet to 3,491 feet. It is also the heaviest traveled. Every Columbus Day, hundreds climb this route during the Greylock Ramble, sponsored by the Adams Chamber of Commerce. The trail has been badly eroded, mostly due to off-road vehicles, which have now been banned here (except for snowmobiles). Cheshire Harbor is the community in the town of Cheshire where the trail actually starts, about 1 mile southeast of where you start.

The unblazed trail leaves as a woods road (Adams Road), heading from the southwest corner of the field. Old walls mark the site. Almost immediately the portion of the trail rising from Cheshire Harbor enters left. Riveted drainage pipes and barbed wire hark back to the time when this road served active farms.

At 11 minutes you come to the first switchback and, in 3 more minutes, to the second, where a trail enters left (ignore it). Soon, depending on the condition of the foliage, you see the summit, with its tower, rising over Peck's Brook ravine. At 17 minutes you round the third switchback and, 4 minutes later, the departure of Old Adams Road makes the fourth. Old Adams Road follows more or less at this contour to the base of Jones's Nose, crossing the AT, which rises from the south. It was a stage route joining Adams and New Ashford; the Jones's farmhouse (no longer standing) served as a stop. Apparently the place was named for the profile of the farmer.

You bear right, staying on the Cheshire Harbor Trail, however, continuing up the moderate grade that characterizes this entire trail. The trail has been blazed blue or orange from time to time, although blazes are not needed. As you rise, the trail erosion diminishes. The northern hardwoods through which you pass are severely stressed, the effect of atmospheric pollution. Scientists have designated plots in the area to study the decline of high altitude forests in New England. The results to date are disturbing. You see many dead birch, beech, and maple. The ledges (left) rise to the ridge that connects Greylock with the next peak south, Saddleball.

At 54 minutes you cross Peck's Brook. Soon a trail drops right to the Gould Farm. Continue on to Rockwell Road, an hour from the car. At this point you join the AT, following its white blazes to the summit. The next stretch parallels the road but is in the woods—which are, suddenly, a boreal, high elevation forest of balsam firs and bogs, through which the trail meanders on bog bridges. The unnamed pond on the left (the highest water body in the state) was dug out of a wet spot by the CCC to serve as a water supply for Bascom Lodge. Beavers are active.

At the three-way road junction (1:08), follow straight ahead, back into the woods. The trail to Peck's Brook Shelter departs across the road, right. You follow the AT, with the old water pipe from the pumphouse on the pond; now the lodge has a drilled well. The next sound you hear may well be the wind in the guy wires of the television and radio broadcast tower, which you pass at 1:14. In three more minutes you pass through the break in the stone walls and come to the War Memorial itself. For those who do not suffer from vertigo, the 92-foot climb up stairs to the lookout is worthwhile, extending your view. It is also worthwhile to tour the summit on ground level, especially looking over the eastern side, directly down to the town of Adams—and, considerably nearer, Greylock Glen.

Remember to start down by the broadcast tower. The road crossings can be confusing, too. Cross the first, staying on the AT. After the second crossing, the AT continues straight (south) while the Cheshire Harbor Trail bears left. The trip down takes just about the same time as up.

Since the summit is the focus of 43 miles of trails in the Greylock Reservation, numerous variations on this basic, east side climb are possible. If you can get someone to serve as chauffeur, an east to west hike across the ridge could begin on the Cheshire Harbor Trail and end on the Hopper Trail. Or, with the aid of a Berkshire Regional Transit Authority bus from North Adams to Cheshire, an east to north climb would link the Cheshire Harbor Trail with the Bellows Pipe Trail. (Hopper and Bellows Pipe Trails are described below.) A loop, eschewing the summit, begins on Cheshire Harbor Trail, follows south on the AT over Saddleball and past the Bassett Brook Campsite to Old Adams Road. Follow left (north) 1.5 miles on Old Adams Road until it joins the Cheshire Harbor Trail again (about 15 miles). Cheshire Harbor Trail and Old Adams Road are ski-able with deep snow cover.

BELLOWS PIPE TRAIL

4 miles (2 hours hiking time) one way

Road approaches

Coming from Williamstown toward North Adams on Route 2, turn south onto Notch Road soon after passing Harriman and West Airport. The road climbs through a residential area and woods, turning sharply left at Mount Williams Reservoir. After 2.4 miles from Route 2, park at the gate, after Notch Road turns right to enter the Mount Greylock State Reservation; Bellows Pipe Trail is the gravel road that headed straight where you turned right, so you must walk down to it. (You can reach the same point via Reservoir Road, also from North Adams, or by Pattison Road, the continuation of Luce Road in Williamstown.)

Camping

You pass a lean-to, a ski shelter, and Bascom Lodge on this hike. The lean-to is a bit more than halfway in time, where the Bellows Pipe Ski Trail meets the Bellows Pipe (hiking) Trail. It faces east. The ski shelter is next to the parking lot at the summit. With multiple stoves in the middle and closed sides, it is meant for day use but is available at night for emergencies in the winter. Bascom Lodge stands firmly on the summit, a warm and cheery destination in summer and early fall.

BELLOWS PIPE TRAIL

Although this trail may be too steep for a comfortable descent (see the end of this description for alternatives), it is hard to think of a better place to be under certain conditions than climbing the Bellows Pipe. One set of conditions is a sunny day on light, powdery snow—on skis. Another is a warm morning, as the fog burns off in the valley, perhaps in late May, when the ephemeral flowers are blossoming and all the brooks are running high. The sun bursts yellow through the trees, suddenly creating shadows where none had been and picking out the dew on the shrubbery.

You are starting at 1,304 feet in elevation and climbing to 3,491. In places, particularly on the Bellows Pipe Ski Trail, the going is steep. As you cross the chain meant to keep vehicles off the road, it's clear you're on North Adams watershed property, which protects Notch Reservoir, an impoundment of the brook that cuts the valley you climb. There are no blazes on city land, which extends almost to the Notch. The large sugar maples beside the gravel road have been there many generations; the pines were planted as a way of having trees beside a reservoir that would not fill the water with leaves. You pass several cellar holes and old walls you probably won't notice if the foliage is out. But you may notice the road was uncommonly well made: edged with stone, built with a crown, ditched on the sides. In places it has been cobbled.

For these and many other man-made features of the route, credit Jeremiah Wilber and his descendants, who cut a spacious and productive farm out of the wilderness of this mountain about 1800, built the first road to the summit, grew hay, boiled off enormous quantities of maple syrup, grazed cattle and sheep, killed marauding wolves and bears, built three mills, and raised a dozen children by two wives.

Yours is the route Henry David Thoreau took in 1844, when he heeded Hawthorne's and Emerson's advice to visit Greylock. (Emerson called it "a serious mountain.") At one of these homes, now a cellar hole, Thoreau stopped to converse with a lady who was combing her long tresses. You can read about it in *A Week on the Concord and Merrimack Rivers*. He spent the night in a wooden tower on the summit. When he awoke, the clouds had closed in below him, and he found himself "in a country such as we might see in dreams, with all the delights of paradise."

In 10 minutes you come to a yarding area used for timber cutting, but continue straight on the unblazed trail. The going gets a bit steeper. Soon, through breaks in the foliage, you can see the ridge of Ragged Mountain (which rises 2,451 feet) to the east, over Notch Brook Valley. The next landmark, at 31 minutes, is a bridge. This area is called Bellows Pipe, a name that Thoreau used. The name presumably derives from the fact that wind rushes through the notch just as air rushes through the pipe at the end of a bellows.

Having crossed a dozen or more tributaries, you finally cross the main stem of Notch Brook at 40 minutes and after a short, very steep eroded section, are in the notch (2,197 feet in elevation), clear not long ago as an orchard. At the site of informal camping under spruces at the left, a marked trail follows the wall up to the cliffs on Ragged. Thoreau may have climbed up there to check his bearings before his final bushwhack to the summit. Now that you are on state land, look for orange and blue blazes that lead to the summit.

Follow a level section, looking down into Adams. At 50 minutes turn right on the blazed trail (the original road continues down to become Gould Road in Adams; see the description of alternate ways home below). The shelter is on your right, almost immediately. You are now on the Bellows Pipe Ski Trail, cut by the CCCs in the 1930s; you will recognize it from the series of steep sharp switchbacks. At 1:02 do not take the unmarked trail straight ahead, which leads to the Thunderbolt. Instead, follow right, on a section that is a real workout if you are on skis. As a matter of fact, it's a workout on foot.

The trees are becoming lower and more scraggly on the steep eastern face—more beech and birch, somewhat stunted. After five switchbacks and testing ascents, you come out at 1:22 on the white-blazed AT, heading south to the summit. Trees are often ice-covered on this stretch in the winter; if you catch them when the sun hits, the effect is of walking through a lighted chandelier. If a breeze is blowing, the branches clink together like cut glass—well, inexpensive glass. Within a minute the AT joins the Thunderbolt Trail for the final assault. If you plan to descend this way, be sure to turn around at this point to check the lay of the land, which can be confusing on the way back. As the Indians said, "Every trail is two trails, one going and one coming." Soon a blue blazed trail heads right, crossing nearby Notch Road to Robinson's Point. You continue on the steep Thunderbolt to cross Summit Road (1:33). The ski shelter the CCC built at the head of the Thunderbolt is right. You skirt the parking lot and arrive at the memorial tower at 1:15.

Remember, if you decide to return by this route, that you start on the AT north, by the parking lot. The AT south takes off by the TV tower actually only partway around the compass. But the Bellows Pipe Ski Trail may be too steep to be a pleasant descent (the knees!), so consider a different way home. In the winter, ski down Notch Road to your car. Leave on Summit Road and turn right at the only intersection. You don't want to walk down a road with traffic in the summer, however, so you might arrange a two-car hike, with someone meeting you at the summit or at the base of another one of the trails described here. Cheshire Harbor, Hopper, and Roaring Brook are good trails down as well as up. A long alternative would be to make a loop by descending the Thunderbolt, again very steep, or the Gould Trail to West Road to Notch Road in Adams (different from the two other Notch roads you've been on), which soon degenerates to a four-wheel vehicle road and meets Reservoir Road at Notch Reservoir. That would add 16 miles to your trip, for a total of 20. In effect, you would make a loop around Ragged; a shorter version would leave out the summit by following straight to Gould Road at the Notch.

THE HOPPER TRAIL

8 miles (3.5 hours hiking time)

Road approaches

Beginning at Field Park in Williamstown, follow Route 2 east to Water Street which becomes Green River Road (.5 mile). Turn right. Hopper Road turns left at Mount Hope Park (2.5 miles). Follow Hopper Road along the brook, past Bressett Road, until it swings left (straight ahead is Potter Road) beyond some open fields. It turns to gravel, ending at a state parking area between the barn and farmhouse (2.75 miles).

Camping

As well as Bascom Lodge at the summit, on this route you hike through Sperry Road Campground, with 34 tent and 5 group sites, including 2 three-sided shelters. There are no showers, no flush toilets, no hookups. The state collects a small fee in season for overnight parking, picnicking, or camping. The Deer Hill shelter, reconstructed by an Eagle Scout and his father, is within .5 mile of the campground. Please note that the Hopper itself is classified as a low impact area: no fires, camping, or vehicles are permitted, except for tent camping at the Haley field, at the beginning of the Money Brook Trail. The Sperry Road Campground is also convenient for the Stony Ledge and Roaring Brook Trails. For reservations at Sperry Road, call 1-877-I-Camp-Ma or www.ReserveAmerica.com.

THE HOPPER TRAIL

This is the classic Greylock hike, from 1,096 feet to the summit, 3,491 feet, on a historic trail, through the deeply eroded "grain hopper" that marks the western side of the Greylock massif. Hopper Road didn't originally end at the gate; instead, it passed between the stone walls you walk between and then forded Money Brook, continuing up the far side into the inner Hopper. The route you are following was originally laid out by Almond Harrison, who pioneered a farm at the campground site about 1800. President Edward Dorr Griffin dismissed his Williams College students from class on a May day in 1830 to improve this road and extend it to the summit, where they built the first tower. At the time, the summit was tree-covered, so the tower was the only alternative to shinnying up the stunted fir trees for a view. Later the CCC built its camp where Harrison's farm had been; still later the state developed its campgrounds in the same spot, as the spruces grew into the once-open fields.

Pass through the farm gate and the state vehicle gate. No free-running dogs or bicycles are allowed. Stroll down the road between the hay fields. Pass the Haley Farm Trail, right, a good way of making a loop with Hopper Trail, to the campgrounds. The Haley Farm Trail goes to the end of Sperry Road, on which the tent sites are located. Leave the old road, which continues as Money Brook Trail, at the sign (8 minutes) for Hopper Trail, bearing right following the blue blazes to the edge of the upper field. There the trail plunges into the woods. For the next quarter mile or so the trail has been carefully engineered to make it as dry as possible.

This steady, no-nonsense rise, cut into the sidehill, was the first leg of the Berkshires-to-the-Cape Bridle Trail, which wandered across the Commonwealth in the late 19th century. The large birch trees seem to have reached the ends of their lives, as beech and maple crowd them out. At 34 minutes, the Money Brook cutoff drops into the valley. You can probably hear the song of Money Brook, floating from the floor. Just shy of an hour you reach Sperry Road and the campground. (Turn right for Stoney Ledge.) Turn left and, in 5 minutes, left again, across from but beyond the contact station, as the Hopper Trail, still blazed blue, leaves the road.

This climb (from here on identical to that described in the Stony Ledge hike) has been moved to avoid erosion, so it is not well worn. Turn left on the Deer Hill Trail, which was once a carriage road (1:15). Note this turn for the return trip. The trail is relatively level and stone-covered, as erosion has removed the thin soil. Where the Overlook Trail exits (1:27), your trail turns steeper. Large trees are less frequent at the higher elevation, giving way to more shrubbery. Nick a corner of Rockwell Road, at a spring, but stick to the woods, which soon turn to spruce. A new section of trail avoids coming out on the road again. From here to the summit, follow the white blazes. You cross swampy areas on footbridges. At 1:35 you pass the pond, no longer used, dug to serve as a water supply for Bascom Lodge. Follow the AT across the road intersection a minute later. Study these road crossings so that you will know what to do on the return trip.

Climb steeply, through fir and spruce, crossing the old water line, for eight minutes until you reach the broadcast tower and two more minutes to the memorial tower (1:46).

For the return, the broadcast tower is the landmark for the proper direction to depart the summit on the AT. At 10 minutes you cross the intersection, still on the AT, even though the "Adams" sign may momentarily confuse you.

You pass the pond. Six more minutes take you to the next road crossing where, instead of following the AT, you turn right, down the road and back into the woods at the "Hopper" sign. Continue on the Deer Hill Trail until the Hopper Trail exits, right (35 minutes). After you turn right on Sperry Road, look for the Hopper Trail angling off to the right. The return trip takes 1:30, for a total travel (no pauses) time of 3:17.

You needn't return the way you came, of course. The most obvious circuit—up the Hopper Trail and down Money Brook—is lengthy if you include the summit: 11 miles, via the AT over Mount Williams to Tall Spruces. After you cross Notch Road, take a left toward the shelter on the Money Brook Trail. You can save more than a mile by cutting off the AT prior to Mount Williams and hiking down the road .5 mile to the cutoff for the Money Brook Trail. Shorter still would be to omit the summit of Greylock—all right to do after you've hit the summit a few times. Take the Hopper Trail to the Overlook Trail. Follow the Overlook Trail until it meets Notch Road. Take Notch Road 100 yards north to the cutoff to the AT on top of the ridge, and continue as described above. This route runs about 8 miles. A more attractive, although steep, shorter (6.5 miles) hike links Money Brook and Prospect Trails.

STONY LEDGE AND ROARING BROOK TRAILS

9 miles (3.75 hours hiking time)

Road approaches

Beginning at Field Park in Williamstown, drive south on Route 7, 5.5 miles to Roaring Brook Road, left just before the Mass Highway garage; alternately, coming from the south, after entering Williamstown, turn right immediately beyond the garage. Drive 1 mile up the gravel road until you see the sign indicating the private Mount Greylock Ski Club. Use the parking area large enough for 5 or 6 cars just downstream from the sign; in the unlikely event that area is filled, you will have to pull over nearer Route 7.

Camping

See the description under "Hopper Trail."

STONY LEDGE TRAIL

You can call this loop Stony Ledge for the first eminence, with its spectacular view of the Hopper, but you actually hike on several other trails: Hopper, Appalachian, and Roaring Brook, for instance. You rise from a deep valley, through the plateau that hosts a campground, to the summit, and back down through a hemlock forest. Both ascent and descent have steep sections. This hike (or Haley Farm Trail: see Hooper Trail) is the most logical one if your goal is to sit on the edge of the abyss at Stony Ledge.

The trailhead is streamside, across from the ski club sign. You begin on a well-established old woods road, blazed blue for the most part, although some of the previous white blazes persist. You cross Roaring Brook on a bridge, beyond the old wagon ford. You climb, passing a trail that rises into the fields, left. After 10 minutes you drop down to the brook again and cross it on a log bridge. The old trail, exiting right, rises to the ski club. At 13 minutes you cross a feeder stream. Just beyond, bear left on Stony Ledge rather than straight on Roaring Brook, on which you will return.

A sign indicates the wide, grassy trail to be an "intermediate ski trail," which refers to downhill skiing. Cross-country skiing here is "advanced." Although you can see how the CCC laid it out wide enough to enable some maneuvering, it hasn't been maintained for skiing.

Soon the trail picks up an old road, which it follows most of the rest of the way. From time to time you will see the telltale charcoal bits indicating charcoal burning sites. The product was used to smelt iron ore until the late 19th century when the Bessemer process came in. At 30 minutes the trail begins to bear left and climb sharply, which it continues to do, with a branch of Roaring Brook left, to the ridge you soon will see to the right. The Haley Farm Trail enters, left.

You arrive at the lean-to at 53 minutes. Walk straight ahead to the gravel turnaround on Sperry Road. Sit and absorb the summit and ridge across the chasm. The morning is not as good a time as evening because of shadows, but on the wall opposite you can see dark stands of red spruce, some nearly 200 years old, probably the oldest stands in the Commonwealth. You can also see March Cataract, to the southeast. It won't be prominent when late summer reduces the water flow, however.

Walk down the road about 1 mile, between azaleas and berry bushes into the camping area. You can easily see why Sperry Road is regarded as the best laid out campground around. Autos stay by the road; campers walk in 50 or 75 feet to the sites, which are separated from one another for privacy. At 1:10 the Hopper Trail enters the road from the left. You see the Roaring Brook Trail entrance, right. At 1:13 the Hopper Trail exits, with you, to the left, a few hundred feet beyond the contact station.

Climb fairly steeply on a well-worn path, still blazed blue, which joins Deer Hill Trail (actually a carriage road), on which you turn left at 1:25. The path is relatively level until the Overlook Trail exits, left (1:37). You are surrounded by the big leaves of the hobble bush, known as the woodsman's toilet paper. You come out on a corner of Rockwell Road but stay to the woods, which soon turn to spruce. A new section of trail avoids coming out on the road again. You cross bridges over swamp. At 1:45 you pass the pond the CCC dug, no longer used. Follow the AT across the road intersection a minute later. Study the layout of these road crossings for the way back.

Eight minutes later you climb steeply to the broadcast tower and 2 minutes later (1:56), the War Memorial Tower. Cross to the east side, drop over the edge a bit, and look down on the cleared fields and ponds of Greylock Glen. Look close, don't they?

The broadcast tower is your landmark for the proper direction to depart the summit on the AT. At 10 minutes you cross the intersection, on the AT, even though the "Adams" sign may momentarily confuse you. You pass the pond. At 10:16, the next road crossing, instead of following the AT, bear right. Turn off the Deer Hill Trail, right, at 35 minutes, beyond the brook, to the campground.

In 42 minutes from the summit (2:38), turn right on Sperry Road and shortly left, where the sign says "Roaring Brook Trail," blazed blue (occasionally white), across a bridge, and right along the brook. The Circular Trail leaves left in 5 minutes, but you cross the bridge; just beyond the bridge the Deer Hill Trail leaves left. Stay with Roaring Brook. You pass through hobble bush, black raspberries, beech, and maple. You descend steadily through hemlock, aware of a brook on each side. The descent becomes steep.

Gradually the two brook branches come closer, as you descend, until you must cross the smaller (3:16). You are at the junction with Stony Ledge Trail. After crossing and attaining some elevation, look down into the scenic, rocky gorge, where you can see the remains of a millrun. Farther downstream, in the day lilies, is the cellar hole for the mill. At 1:35 from the summit or 3:31 round trip you will be back at your starting point.

Skiers should do the loop by climbing Roaring Brook to Sperry Road and returning via Stony Ledge. Hikers go the opposite direction purely for the aesthetic satisfaction of coming out at the end of the climb on Stony Ledge. They might prefer the 3-mile shorter version, however, omitting the summit. In season, the hike could be spiced up with a visit to March Cataract or Deer Hill Falls. You can link all other Greylock trails to these two, for two-car variations on this hike.

WILLIAMSTOWN

Soldiers at Fort Massachusetts, once located where the Price Chopper supermarket now resides on Route 2 in North Adams, built the first homes in the township west of the fort and held their first Proprietors' Meeting there in 1753. Then a flare-up of the French and Indian War drove them out; of the original residents only Benjamin Simonds returned, with a wife and daughter, after having been in prison in Quebec. Rachel Simonds was the first child of European stock born in the area. The Simonds River Bend Tavern still stands, beautifully restored, run now as a bed and breakfast, on Simonds Road (Route 7 north of town).

Diminished as a farming town, Williamstown is more famous for the college that has grown up with it. Ephraim Williams Jr. was a commander at the fort; on his way to battle at Lake George in 1755, he rewrote his will to establish a secondary school for the children of his command. Town and school were named for his generosity. The trustees converted his school into Williams College, which opened in 1793.

The college has attracted to the community the Clark Art Institute, with its ravishing collections of French Impressionists and 19th-century American artists and sculptors, and the Williamstown Theatre Festival, busy all summer with myriad main stage and experimental productions, readings, and cabarets. Both have been singled out by tough critics as the best of their kinds in the United States.

So, should the weather turn sour, despair not. The Clark (open seven days in the summer) provides an eyeful that can last all day. Other undercover destinations: the Williams College Museum of Art, the Hopkins Forest Farm Museum, the Chapin Rare Books Library, and the planetarium show at the Old Hopkins Observatory (reservations required). As well as shopping on Spring and Water Streets, visitors may take self-guided tours of the Williams College campus, by studying the map at Hopkins Hall, off Main Street.

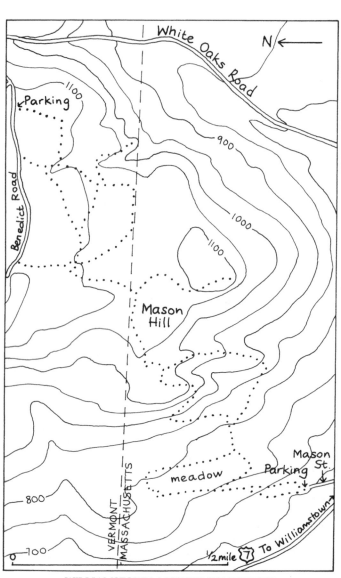

WILLIAMSTOWN: MOUNTAIN MEADOW

WALKS

MOUNTAIN MEADOW

Various trails

This delightful property of The Trustees of Reservations can be reached from Route 7 north of Williamstown center or from Pownal, Vermont, via White Oaks Road in Williamstown, depending on the landscape you seek. To reach open fields with a side trip to a wooded lookout, follow Route 7 north to Mason Street, the steep, gravel road across from the Chef's Hat. The TTOR parking lot is at the end. Ticks, including deer ticks that carry Lyme disease, have been rife in the fields recently, so tuck your pant legs into your socks and check yourself after walking.

To get to a second-growth wooded area, sprouting from former gravel pits, with a side trip to a higher lookout, take Route 7 north to North Hoosac Road, turning right across from the sign for the town's DPW facilities. Take the second left (north) on White Oaks Road for .5 mile, where the road turns gravel at the Vermont line. Continue on up the hill, bearing left, for a few hundred yards. Go straight on Benedict Road rather than right. The TTOR parking lot is soon on the left.

A large map at each parking lot shows the trails and often small maps are available for the taking. All the blazes are yellow. From the Benedict Road lot, try walking to the cabin site, about 25 minutes each way. The cabin burned but the chimney remains. The views are mostly of Williamstown and the Taconics. From the extreme west side of the lookout you can see Greylock. Mountain Meadow is a fine, rolling site for cross-country skiing.

STONE HILL

1.5 miles (1 hour)

For Williamstown's favorite walk, drive south on South Street, beginning at Field Park, across from the Williams Inn. At .5 mile, turn right into the Clark Art Institute and left, not following the road to the Stone Hill Center but swinging around behind the main building to a parking lot. (The Clark plans a new campus but will continue to direct walkers to Stone Hill Trails.)

This leisurely stroll will take you from the Clark parking lot, 750 feet in elevation, on a meandering path through old-growth northern hardwood forest, to a stone seat at 1,000 feet; then down through open fields for a striking view before returning to the lot.

To find the trailhead, look for two small gravestones that mark the eternal resting place of dogs that belonged to a previous owner of the property, Dr. Vanderpool Adriance. Sterling and Francine Clark purchased his land and built the white marble building for their home and art collection. It was opened to the public in 1955. The darker building to the right was added to the institute in 1973. The original trail and footbridge were built in 1985, the institute's 30th anniversary. The trails, with their clear signs, pass through a variety of birch, beech, and maple stands, as well as some hemlock and pine, so a walker can compare and enjoy, working gradually uphill.

Take the Howard Path over the footbridge, following signs to "Woodland Trails," "Stone Bench Trail," and white, diamond-shaped markers. At about 15 minutes, note a signed trail that turns right to the open fields you will pass through later. You continue straight to the remains of the colonial Stone Hill Road, which preceded Route 7 as the main north-south route in the county. The road has been improved as access to the town's water tank, buried under a field. Follow up the hill to the stone seat erected as a memorial to George Moritz Wahl, a professor of German at Williams College who was incorrectly suspected by some of being a German spy

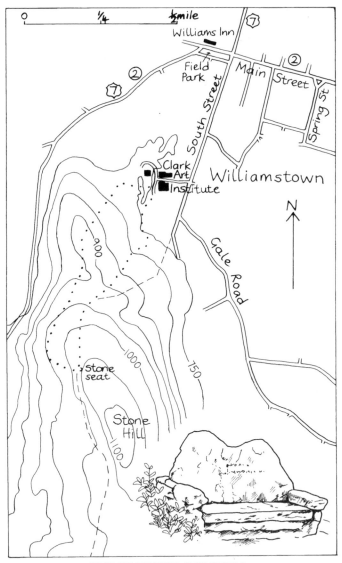

WILLIAMSTOWN: STONE HILL

during World War I. He was accustomed to climbing to this spot in the evening to watch the sunset—in those days the fields were open. This monument was the town's apology and tribute.

This is the far point of the hike, but you might like to continue south on the old road, to see how the hill got its name. If you look through the trees to your left, you will see the schist outcroppings. After returning, walk through the gate across from the seat, carefully closing it behind you because cows may be pasturing in the fields. (Cows are curious enough to look you over but are harmless.) Head down, following the open land as it swings right. Although the trail remains clear, it passes through a short stretch of forest, emerging at the head of a long, sloping field. Set your sights to the right of a clump of trees on the ridge ahead, dipping down and then rising to a view that includes the Clark, Main Street and the college, the Dome in southern Vermont, East Mountain (encompassing Pine Cobble and Eph's Lookout), the Hoosac Valley heading into North Adams, the Hoosac Range beyond the city, and the Greylock Range. The ridge is the ideal picnic site on this trip. You can keep the view in sight as you wander down the field, skirting a wet area.

Follow across the next field, heading down the hill to the wooden gate. Note: you are now part of the view for museum-goers. Perhaps you are being compared to the pastoral subject of an old master. Act accordingly. You are passing above what was called a "haw-haw" in the 18th century. This device enclosed stock by a ditch, although the fence that would have been visible at the bottom has been moved to the edge of the parking lot.

Picnic tables rest under the trees around the parking lot. In the summer months a cafe serves light lunches in the newer building, if that fits your strolling plans. Longer walks are possible. The Taconic Golf Course, across South Street, is also open for cross-country skiing.

Many other strolls in town are yours for the walking. The description of the Triple-R Brooks Trail tells you how to get to a collection of them in Hopkins Forest. Walking

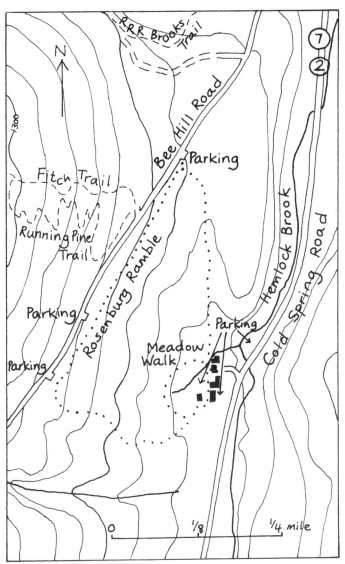

WILLIAMSTOWN: SHEEP HILL

guides to the town, available at the Williams Inn or at the information booth nearby, show numerous strolls that also reveal something of the history of Williamstown.

WILLIAMSTOWN RURAL LANDS TRAILS

Several options: up to 3.3 miles (2 hours)

SHEEP HILL/FITCH TRAILS

The Williamstown Rural Lands Foundation has established its headquarters and education center at the old Rosenburg farm at Sheep Hill, 2 miles south of the town center on Routes 7 and 2. (Look for a sign and driveway on right just south of Fisheries and Wildlife Hemlock Brook access.) Ample parking beyond the farmhouse. A kiosk is full of information about the property and other Williamstown walking venues. The farm is redolent of fond memories for continuing small-scale dairying almost to the end of the 20th century, for serving as a ski area, and for the warmth and wisdom of Rosenburg family members.

The 1.5-mile Rosenburg Ramble tours the perimeter of the property, beginning on the north side of the buildings. The Meadow Walk, leaving from the south side of the buildings, is a brief tour of the mown fields. Those who want to include a walk in the woods can begin the Ramble, cross Bee Hill Road at the second cleared lookout, and follow the Fitch Trail either to the summit of Bee Hill or all the way to the RRR Brooks Trail; go back to Bee Hill Road at the bridge, and then up the road to the first lookout, returning to complete the Ramble. While the views are better from the open fields than the summit of Bee Hill, you will find there some magnificent sugar maples, some over 6 feet in diameter. The Fitch and RRR Brooks Trails (see the descriptions below) are blazed blue.

HIKES

BERLIN MOUNTAIN

5.25 miles (3 hours hiking time)

Road approaches

From Field Park at the Williams Inn in Williamstown, drive south on Routes 7 and 2 for 2.5 miles until they diverge. Follow Route 2 west (right). A half mile up the hill, turn left on Torrey Woods Road. Follow straight at the bottom of the hill onto a gravel road, sometimes called Bee Hill and sometimes Berlin. From the point at which a closed road enters to the right, it is part of a 1799 post road between Boston and Albany. Bear left at the fork, climbing past a few houses to a small (four-car) parking area on the left. Blue trail blazes head into the woods 150 yards back down the road.

Alternatively, you can continue .5 mile to the old Williams College ski area and leave your car there. The route you will be taking comes out at the ski area.

Although Hemlock Brook looks pristine, you should carry your own water on this, and all, hikes. At the junction of Routes 7 and 2, Margaret Lindley Park, a town-owned swimming area, provides a pond with water diverted from Hemlock Brook, changing rooms with plumbing, snack machines, and lifeguards.

BERLIN MOUNTAIN

From the parking area to the summit is a demanding hike, ascending from 1,400 feet (probably 100 feet lower in the ravines), across two branches of Hemlock Brook and directly up the side of the ridge to an altitude of 2,798 feet in 2.5 miles. Members of the Williams Outing Club originally laid out the trail in 1933—clearly they were a no-nonsense group. The remainder of your trip, down into the pass and down the post road, is fairly easygoing. The

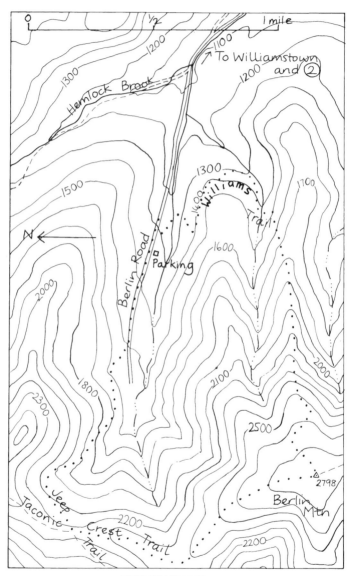

BERLIN MOUNTAIN

reward is an unusual 360-degree view, in clear weather everything from Mount Greylock to the Adirondacks. You see some land-use history, as well as sampling old-growth hemlock woods and hardwood forests of more recent vintage. Blueberrying is good here in July and August.

Wear layered clothing, because the wind on the summit is apt to be cool, particularly if you decide to take in the sunset. There are wet as well as steep spots in the hike, and brook crossings, so wear hiking boots.

The wet spots begin as you follow easterly to an old woods road for five minutes until turning right to cross the first branch of Hemlock Brook. Be particularly vigilant for the blue blazes at both brook crossings. Scramble up the far side, jogging right and left as the trail jumps from one logging road to another. This part, a 1980 rerouting to avoid private property, is a bit hard to follow, as it doesn't seem to be tending in any direction. Soon, however, you start up a steep logging road and turn left over the ridge and down to the outing club's former cabin site, at about .5 hour. Misuse of the old trail and cabin led the landowner to request the cabin be razed and the trail rerouted: the moral is obvious.

After a sharp right turn, the trail drops down to cross the second branch of Hemlock Brook. Scrambling up the other side you turn right on a broad woods road, following the brook west. Back on this older portion, the trail is easier to follow. Soon it leaves the road and begins a steep ascent up the side of the valley, leveling out and joined by a red-blazed trail at about an hour. This trail rises from the former Carmelite property and accompanies the 1933 trail to the summit. Stay alert, because recent logging has altered this section. Look back from time to time during the climb for views of Greylock.

At 1:25 a hemlock grove across the valley on the other side of the mountain provides a lovely view of the Dome and East Mountain with its Pine Cobble. Then the trail rises steeply once again until it joins the upper end of the college's downhill ski trail. Turn uphill (left) for the brief distance to the windswept summit (1:30). The four concrete piers once anchored a fire tower. Blueberries and raspberries surround you; this is an excellent picnic site. To the east the Greylock massif broods over Williamstown. The ski runs you see to the south are cut on the sides of Jiminy Peak. If the weather is clear enough, you may be able to pick out the Catskills to the southwest and the Adirondacks to the northwest—perhaps even the capitol buildings in Albany. To the northeast rise the Green Mountains of Vermont. You are standing in the township of Berlin in New York State, looking directly down into the valley of the Little Hoosic, which threads through Berlin and Petersburgh. If it is noon, you may hear one bark of the fire siren in Berlin.

The Taconic Crest Trail (TCT) goes off to the south and north. It is marked by diamond-shaped white blazes, in most cases imposed on a blue square. You will hardly need them, however, as you follow north the deeply rutted jeep trail, once the access road to the fire tower. (Detours around large puddles might be momentarily confusing.) After 20 minutes you approach the pass. The former post road, a surfaced section you were driving on, rises from Berlin, to the west. You can see the TCT continuing up the slopes of the open ridge to Petersburgh Mountain, straight ahead. To the east the badly eroded post road descends to the start of the hike. You may want to linger in this area to enjoy the view of Williamstown, to pick the blueberries, or to picnic. The trail bikes and jeeps that come through the intersection can be annoying; however, the state of New York has acquired much of the land along the Taconic Crest in this area and has imposed controls on off-road vehicles.

Turn right down the post road for 1 mile. You soon cross near the origin of one branch of Hemlock Brook, high in a mountain spring. Immediately to the right of the trail is a foundation for Alexander Walker's early 19th-century tollgate farmhouse. After about 15 minutes, look left to see the old stone marker at the state line, also leftover from post road days. From the college ski area, it is .5 mile down the road to where you began your hike, three hours of hiking altogether.

An alternative route, shorter but harder on the legs, would be to descend the ski run from the summit to the parking area. Or, if two cars are available, you might consider leaving one at Petersburgh Pass, on Route 2. The distance from Berlin Pass to Petersburgh Pass, 1.5 miles, is the same as from Berlin Pass to the parking area. A less strenuous outing, although still a hike rather than a walk, would begin at the heights of Petersburgh Pass, climb most of Petersburgh Mountain (Mount Raimer), and end down at the college ski area.

Brook crossing, Berlin Mountain

PINE COBBLE AND BROAD BROOK TRAILS

Williamstown and Pownal, Vermont, 10 miles (5 hours hiking time), plus 3 miles to complete loop

Road approaches

From Field Park in Williamstown, drive north on Route 7, over the Hoosic River at the bottom of the hill, and right at the first turn, North Hoosac Road. Follow that past Cole Avenue. Turn left on Pine Cobble Road to a parking lot, left. The trail begins across the road from the lot. It is marked with an informative sign. With the addition of 3 miles to the total trip, you can make this hike a loop; otherwise, you will want to leave a second car at the Broad Brook trailhead. To get there: backtrack on North Hoosac until Bridges Road bears right. Follow that to White Oaks Road. Turn right again. Follow White Oaks to the Vermont line, where the road surface becomes gravel. Park in the area just to your right over the line.

Camping

The Seth Warner shelter, a three-sided, Adirondack-style lean-to, is a destination. The local chapter of the Green Mountain Club keeps it well maintained, with firewood and a clean privy. A tent camping area is nearby. Although Broad Brook serves the city of North Adams for drinking water, it is still safer to carry your own. Sand Springs Pool (slightly farther west on Bridges Road than White Oaks Road) is a private swimming spa open to the public for a fee.

PINE COBBLE AND BROAD BROOK TRAILS

Pine Cobble is one of the most popular climbs in Williamstown, but few hikers venture north along the ridge to Eph's Lookout; traffic beyond there is mostly Long Trail

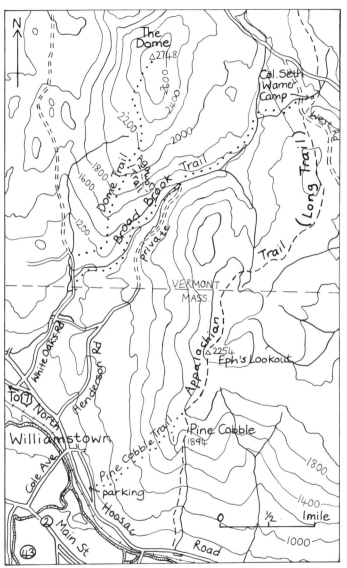

WILLIAMSTOWN: PINE COBBLE/BROAD BROOK/THE DOME

View from Eph's Lookout: Pine Cobble over Broad Brook Valley

or AT through-hikers. Although the lower end of Broad
Brook Trail sees many hikers, the upper end is only slightly
used, in part because it is tough going. This hike covers
East Mountain, the hunk that, located mostly in Vermont
together with the Dome, makes up the north skyline from
Williamstown. The route contrasts hiking a highland
plateau (1,880 to 2,000 feet in elevation) with following the
rocky, mountain stream as it knifes down 1,000 feet. Views
out are excellent toward the beginning of the trip. Views in,
later, include several glacial erratics, towering hemlock, and
mossy brook chasms. From the Vermont line the AT and the
Long Trail are one to Rutland.

After climbing the bank across from the parking lot, you
follow parallel to the road and into the woods. As you climb
moderately, you can look back to see the Hoosic River and
the town. The trail shows some gravel and sand, evidence
of the hill being shore to a glacial lake 10,000 years ago.

After 20 minutes you start climbing steeply for another

10 minutes to the top of a plateau on scree (loose accumulation of stone). The second-growth birch and oak, in poor soil conditions, are thin and small. At about 34 minutes, bear left where a former trail enters right. The trail gradually increases in angle until (44 minutes) you pass a large boulder on the left, a resting point for many a weary hiker. Then the trail climbs steeply to the ridge. Turn right and follow any one of the paths for three minutes to the quartzite rock pile for which, together with the prevailing tree species, Pine Cobble was named (1,894 feet).

You are looking at Mount Williams reservoir and mountain—one of the Greylock peaks. You overlook Williamstown and, to the east, North Adams, in the valley. The Hoosacs rise farther east and the Taconics, west. You are standing on the southern extremity of the Green Mountains. Behind you, in that dark valley of Sherman Brook, rises the AT, which you will meet later on, unless you decide to descend as you came up, for a 3.2-mile jaunt and view. The route from here on is both more remarkable and challenging than the standard day hike.

Backtrack to the trail junction. If you decide to continue, instead of descending, follow the blue blazes north, winding through scrawny growth, past a bolt that once anchored a utility pole (1:02). The vegetation opens up at a burn area, now covered with blueberries. Blazes are painted on stone; look for some cairns as well. The highest pile of loose stone (1:10) is Eph's Lookout (2,254 feet), named for the college's benefactor, soldier of the king, Ephraim Williams, who probably never stood where you do. The Hoosac Valley links the communities of Williamstown and Pownal below you. The dwarfed pitch pine behind the rocks are at their northern extent. The AT enters right almost immediately, with several handsome signs: Williamstown, 2.1 miles; Route 2, 2.7 miles south; Vermont line, 1.3 miles north. Follow the white blazes north, into the woods.

The vegetation is beginning to pick up an evergreen flavor: some spruce and white pine. Ignore the trail that enters left (1:29). Occasional lumbering roads cross from now on.

At 1:45 you hit the Vermont border and the beginning of the Long Trail, duly signed. Only 263 miles to Canada! Add your name to the register. You may want to sign with your trail name, as AT through-hikers do.

Although you are on a plateau, it is cut by ravines and sprinkled with boulders (erratics) left by the glaciers. One is nearly a balancing rock. You venture in Green Mountain National Forest, yet much of the land you are passing through belongs to the city of North Adams as watershed. Parallel logs form the pathway through bogs. At 2:29 a woods road crosses. Scrambling up the far, steep side, you arrive on a ledge with a deep ravine right. After another section that may remind you of spruce bogs much farther north, you arrive at the gravel West Road from Clarksburg (2:49). Ignore, temporarily, blue blazes heading north along the road.

Instead, follow straight on the AT/Long Trail for .2 mile until another blue-blazed side trail heads left to the Seth Warner Shelter (3 miles), elevation 2,000 feet. Warner was a patriot and leader of the Green Mountain Boys in the American Revolution. This form of immortality is perpetuated by those folks, GMC members and hikers, who take good care of the shelter. A good spot for a picnic or the night.

Backtrack to West Road and follow the blue blazes. The blue-blazed Broad Brook Trail departs the road just before the culvert through which the brook passes (3:14) and follows the brook, losing elevation at a steady rate. This trail section is not bushed out consistently. At 3:22 you arrive at the first of numerous brook crossings, followed by a very steep ascent on the far side, into a hemlock forest. Just as rapidly you drop down over a promontory between two brook branches (3:31), making your second and third brook crossings. Pay attention to the blazes, especially at stream crossings, and expect sudden shifts in direction. Follow the side for a ways, leaving the stream on your left before yet another steep ascent. If your legs are logy from the exertion so far, you may begrudge these ascents; but there just isn't room for the trail by the brook.

You are starting to find the innumerable logging roads in this area, but follow the blazes over the fourth branch brook crossing (3:50) and then up! again. In five minutes you come out on what was clearly once a road and soon, as further evidence of the lumbering activity, the stone remains of a mill and tail race, the route made for the water to flow from the wheel back to the brook (4:02). You cross that waterway for the fifth crossing. You see the remains of an old wagon, said to have served the lumbermen as a chuck wagon. Directly across the brook is the end of Henderson Road (here just a woods road). You make your sixth stream crossing, but instead of taking Henderson, continue downstream, south side, and up the steep sidehill. At 4:13, make your seventh crossing, followed in 10 minutes by the eighth and last. The Agawon Trail leaves from the far side to rise to the Dome Trail.

At 4:50 you follow a new trail, avoiding the public water supply building, and in four minutes you arrive at the parking area where, if you didn't leave a vehicle, you probably wish you had. After all, you just completed nearly 5 hours of hiking, with a great deal of up and down.

If you are afoot, turn left on White Oaks Road, follow down to the intersection with Bridges Road, turn left, following Bridges—which becomes North Hoosac—back to your point of departure.

As well as choosing to return back down Pine Cobble, you could have made a loop with the AT, ending up on Massachusetts Avenue in Blackinton, a village in the city of North Adams. Or you could have continued past the Seth Warner cutoff, ending up .5 mile later on County Road, (barely) drivable in the summer and a place to leave a car if you wished to do half the trip only. To get to County Road, take Route 7 north in Pownal to Barber's Pond Road. Follow right, past the pond. The road turns sharp right and then sharp left. Turn right immediately on a gravel road. Bear left at the fork.

If you left your car at the base of Pine Cobble and are walking the complete route, taking Henderson Road from the chuck wagon would save you 1 mile of road hiking. Henderson Road in Vermont crosses private property and is closed to all vehicles.

RRR BROOKS TRAIL

8 miles (3.5 hours hiking time), plus .5 mile to complete loop

Road approaches

From Field Park in Williamstown, follow West Main Street down, up, and down to a right turn on Northwest Hill Road, past the end of Bulkley Street; go left into a parking lot on the Hopkins Forest drive. You can begin and end your trip here. To save walking the last segment on Northwest Hill Road, you could leave a second car at a small pullover on Petersburgh Road (the continuation of West Main), at a footbridge, left, where the Hatton Trail comes out. Parking on Bee Hill, which would reduce the trip by 2 miles, is possible at the Sheep Hill Overlook, .5 mile from the junction of Bee Hill with Routes 7 and 2, south of Field Park. For an even shorter version, missing out on Flora Glen, leave a car on Route 2 across from the gate to Taconic Trail State Park.

Camping

The Williams Outing Club cabin in Hopkins Forest is available through the club to people associated with Williams College. It has a wood stove, running water, and a sleeping loft. No other shelters or camping are available on this route. Buxton Gardens, the re-creation of a 19th-century flower garden; the Barn Museum, with displays about farming; and the exhibits in the Rosenburg Center, all at the beginning of this hike, are worth a visit. Hopkins Forest, a 2,500-acre tract bordering New York and Vermont, is an ecology laboratory for Williams College. Please do not wander off the trails because you might inadvertently disturb experiments. Signs explain some of the work in progress, much of which currently has to do with monitoring the effects of acid rain on trees. As alternatives to this route, many strolls, other hikes, and ski tours beckon in Hopkins Forest. Pocket maps are available at the large map near the barn.

RRR BROOKS TRAIL

Although this hike is called the Triple-R Brooks Trail, actually it travels six or seven trails. It's a vigorous outing; you climb from 800 feet to 2,200 feet. As well as evidence of

Petersburgh Valley, RRR Brooks Hike

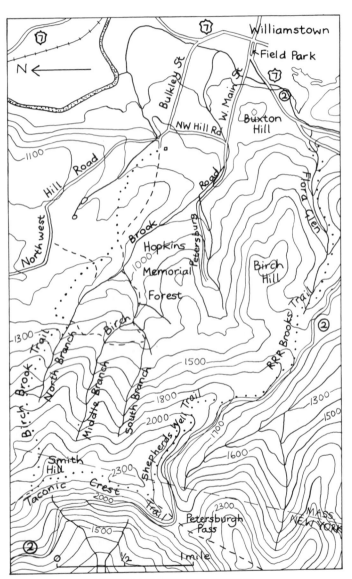

WILLIAMSTOWN: RRR BROOKS

past land use, you view two spectacular brook valleys and, standing 300 feet above the highway, get an eagle's eye look at the old Petersburgh Pass ski area, Berlin Mountain, the Hopper on Greylock, and the Williamstown valley. Remember that cold comes with altitude and that the Taconic Ridge can be extremely windy. On the other hand, standing on the top of this piece of the world in snow and ice crystals is unforgettable. Azaleas and blueberries are found here in season. Equally exciting, the three states, Williams College, and Williamstown are cooperating to create a public recreation area for 3,500 acres in this area.

Beginning at the Hopkins Forest lot, walk up the private drive to the barn. Turn right, past the WOC cabin and the maple sugar house. Continue on this woods road, well made by the CCC when the U.S. Forestry Service ran an experimental forest here. Pass without entering a weather station (4 minutes) that gathers important information for experiments in the forest. Looking down to your right, you will soon see Ford Glen, in the chasm it has cut for itself.

You are on what is known as the Loop Trail. Bear right at the first intersection (18 minutes) and straight at the second (23 minutes). You gradually gain elevation through second-growth birch and maple—all this land was open fields two generations ago. Bear left where a private trail enters right (33 minutes). Just before the brook crossing, turn right on the Birch Brook Trail (36 minutes), blazed blue.

After the broad and carefully constructed Loop Trail, Birch Brook Trail appears indistinguishable in places from a streambed; nevertheless, follow at a moderate rise for 4 minutes. Then turn right, up the side of a shoulder. This trail soon follows the remains of a stone wall, swings left on top of the rise, and another wall and forest boundary appear right. The large maples here were never cut because they were (and are) line trees, marking a property boundary.

At 50 minutes the trail crosses a spring, beginning a steep, steady ascent to the ridge on the left. The forest is older, although the birches and maples are not healthy. You think you've been climbing pretty hard, yet if you look sharp, on your left, you see a cellar hole within spitting distance of the trail. It wasn't just that people farmed these ridges, they lived on them. If you lived up here, you'd think twice about going back to town because you forgot to pick up a spool of thread at the store.

Climbing over phyllite outcrops, after watching your elevation approach the ridge's for some time, at last (1:18) you attain the Taconic Crest Trail (TCT), blazed white. Make a hard left at the yellow sign. Wheeled vehicles are not allowed. You are in New York, .5 mile south of the Vermont border, which juts .5 mile west of Massachusetts's. A *New Yorker* cartoon (1989) showed a real estate broker greeting hikers at the three-state marker .75 mile to the northeast.

Although the vegetation along the crest is thin, due to wind and soil conditions, there are no views from this section of trail. To remedy the situation, climb to the open expanse of Smith Hill, spotted with white quartz outcrops, by taking a largely unmarked trail (1:26) off to the left. With a little luck you'll be able to follow the route in a loop back to the TCT. (This side trip is not included in elapsed time.)

Continue south on the TCT. Signs and blue blazes warn of the Shepherd's Well Trail, left at 1:41. Take it. Farmer Shepherd dug a well, still extant, nearby—another sign of high altitude farming. You will soon confirm you're on the trail by seeing Hopkins Forest postings to your left. Work up the sidehill. Where the trail may appear to go straight through a clearing (1:46), it actually angles left along a ridge. Soon (1:53), you break out into steep-sloping blueberry bushes, high over the highway (Route 2), facing the old Petersburgh Pass ski area now owned by the New York State Department of Environmental Conservation. As you work your way around a shoulder, you see Berlin Mountain, with the telltale streak of the old Williams College ski trail, and the fields rising to the Hopper on Mount Greylock. Winter wind and ice can be a problem here, obscuring the trail, which soon returns into the woods.

You work down at first gradually and then steeply, coming out on an old cut, where trees were once removed to let

telephone wires through (2:01). The wires are gone now.
Turn left, downhill, a couple hundred yards, then right
(2:06) on a wide and grassy logging road, which soon
(2:08) joins the Triple-R Trail. Dean of the College R. R. R.
Brooks laid out the trail, largely on existing old roads.
For example, the trail here appears to have been on
Petersburgh Road before the lower Taconic Trail State
Highway was built in the 1930s. Brooks dug the lowest
part of the trail out of the sidehill, by hand.

For a ways you follow a wall, left. There are azaleas
along this stretch. At 2:23 jog left on old Petersburgh
Road (gravel) and then right, to come out on an old farm
field the state mows occasionally, part of Taconic Trail
State Park. Here is the gate, across from which you might
have spotted a car. (Follow the road up the knoll for an
alternative route to Bee Hill Road.) The run across this
field on skis can be exciting; at other times of the year follow the beaten path through the brush for the corner farthest down. The clump of trees to the left marks a cellar
hole.

Back in the woods (2:32), follow a shoulder between
two rivulets. Following RRR Brooks, cross a bridge at a
boggy area (2:36). Flora Glen, which you keep on the left
for the rest of this hike, may be named not for a person
but for plants. Dropping moderately, in 10 minutes you
cross a second bridge, soon entering a lovely hemlock
forest. The trees find it difficult to cling to the steep valley walls, as storms hurl them, roots and all, into the valley. Western Massachusetts's foremost early poet,
William Cullen Bryant, may have been inspired by the
wild romanticism of Flora Glen. Eventually the trail
drops right into the streambed (2:50), where the going
can be wet and difficult. Then it climbs the valley walls,
on a narrow ledge, and drops to cross the stream on a bog
bridge. In 12 more minutes you come to the foot of the
trail where you see the log home built by Dean Brooks,
and the remains of a dam and early reservoir for the town
of Williamstown. At this point, you can head out to Bee Hill

Road or head up the sidehill on the Hatton Trail, marked with yellow diamonds, to Petersburgh Road and Hopkins Forest, about 2 miles.

It is possible to ski this route on cross-country skis, in the same direction. It can be tough climbing Birch Brook, and the Flora Glen section requires good control. A pleasant stroll would take you on either the shorter or longer (3 miles) Loop Trail in Hopkins Forest. It is possible to park your car at Petersburgh Pass to hike the TCT north to the Snow Hole, allowing the automobile to gain most of the altitude for you.

THE DOME

Pownal, Vermont, 5.2 miles (3 hours hiking time)

Road approaches

Although located in Vermont, the Dome is accessible by road only from Williamstown. (See the map for the Pine Cobble and Broad Brook Trails p.181.) From Field Park, drive north on Route 7 across the Hoosic River. Take the first right onto North Hoosac Road and the second left onto White Oaks Road. Follow White Oaks until you have gone about 4 miles from Field Park. At the Vermont line the road turns to gravel; immediately on your right is a parking lot that also serves the Broad Brook Trail. You can park here or drive another quarter mile to the Dome trailhead, on the right.

Sand Springs Pool (left at the junction of Sands Springs and Bridges roads) is a private spa open to the public for a fee. There are no shelters on this trail. The trail is unusual in that water is available almost the entire route. Still, it is better to carry your own.

THE DOME

The Dome, at 2,748 feet, is a favorite hike of the few who know it, especially in cool weather when its rocky crest reflects the sun and in the winter when its highest vegetation is spectacularly snow- or ice-covered. Although the mountain lies in Vermont, it is distinctly a part of the northern Berkshire skyline, like the East Mountain that borders the north of Williamstown. As the trail dead ends, you must come back down the way you went up. From the parking lot at about 1,000 feet, it is a steady climb; nowhere overwhelming, but demanding. The bald stone summit is unusual, although the view is gradually being obscured by the spruce fringe growing up around it. But the Dome joins only Greylock in this collection of hikes in that you climb out of a second-growth mixed hardwood forest into a distinctly different environment: a Laurentian plateau of spruce and fir bogs of the kind found in northern Canada.

The times in this description assume that you leave your car at the Broad Brook trailhead. Continue up White Oaks Road, gravel now. Pass the small reservoir; the woods road up the Dome leaves to the right after five minutes, beside a branch of Broad Brook. If you miss the trailhead you will soon come to a division of White Oaks Road: a woods road continuing straight, passing through wild country.

Back on the trail—vehicles drive into former fields, growing over, that have served as a logging yard and occasionally as a party site. The Williams Outing Club once blazed the trail white; more recently, red. The trail is broad and blazes clear. One stone of a small family cemetery stands on a knoll to the right: "Polly 1830," it reads. Continue on the old lumber road, bearing right, out of the second field into the woods, at eight minutes.

The road begins a moderate climb along the shoulder of the Broad Brook Valley, passing through a gap in a stone wall at 13 minutes and continuing up at a steady rate until the first terrace, about 5 minutes later. The lumber road, closed by a boulder, goes straight; you should follow the trail left for 15 minutes of strenuous hiking, with occasional detours around the most seriously eroded sections. Erosion, particularly from motorized vehicles, is severe in this section.

The Agawon Trail drops off to the right, down to join the Broad Brook Trail. Just beyond is Meeting House Rock, a large boulder halfway to the summit. And just beyond that, the trail emerges on the second terrace, an open area where azaleas bloom with haunting fragrance in late spring. The trail rises more gently, swinging westerly. The quartzite ledges are covered in some places with gravel and even white sand, left over from the time when the sides of the Dome, like all northern Berkshire ridges, were shore to a glacial lake that inundated the valley to a height of 1,300 feet or more. The deposits left by the glaciers formed the shoulders and plateaus so evident on the Dome, creating a situation typical of Berkshire climbs: the steepest part is at the beginning (you've done it), followed by a leveling or series of plateaus, and ending with a steep but short scramble to the summit.

Surprise: at about one hour, an old Chevy truck stares balefully at you. Presumably someone drove it up the logging road that enters from the left, where it died. Turn right on this road, past intimidating signs that aim to control hunting, not hiking on the trail. Bear left where the logging road continues straight, up a short steep section to the third terrace. Few motorized vehicles get beyond this point.

Now begins a pattern of emerging on successively wetter terraces and bearing right up the slope after attaining each one. After a short ascent to the fourth terrace, angle right for another short ascent to the fifth terrace. The trail begins to follow a brook. Turn right for the ascent to the sixth terrace, and right again to the seventh. Cross the brook. Then back across it, right, to the eighth and last terrace. Have you kept count? Turn right through spruce and fir forest to the rocky ridge.

Follow the ridge to the false summit (1:15): there is no view because of vegetation. Still following the blazes, push through the fir down into a bog, similar in ecology to what you might find hundreds of miles north. Scramble up the quartzite outcroppings to the ridge that leads to the real summit. The blazes are now painted on the rocks, augmented by a few cairns. You will know the summit because there isn't any more up (1:30). Furthermore, you get the first real views: west to the tops of the Taconics and southeast to the Hairpin Turn and the Hoosacs. The view of Greylock is pretty well obscured by spruce now, although an ice storm may improve visibility one of these winters.

When descending, while still on the summit ridge, note the blazes and bear left where it appears the trail continues straight. As well, on the way down remember to turn left at the Chevy. The trip back to the parking lot will take about 1:20, for a three-hour round trip.

An alternative route, either going or coming, would be to use the Agawon Trail between the Dome and Broad Brook Trails. It is steep and requires a stream crossing troublesome at high water. Pretty near the entire Dome Trail is skiable, except for the two summits.

NORTH ADAMS

North Adams was formed from Adams's rib in 1878, as an immediate result of the railroad coming through the Hoosac Tunnel into the north part of Adams—which then outstripped the south part. The incision was already there, though, created by a military line for recruiting soldiers for the Revolutionary War, and based on topography. The Hoosic River floodplains of the southern part lent themselves more to agriculture; the swift falling streams of the north part more to industry.

The slack in employment when the textile mills moved to the southern United States was taken up by the electronics industry, especially during World War II. But after the war, electronics, too, gradually faded. More recently, in the 1980s, the state has tried to help. It created Western Gateway Heritage State Park, an effort to revitalize the downtown by building a memorial to the railroad past and a home for shops and restaurants. The state purchased Natural Bridge, a marble span carved by a stream, from private interests. And the state worked with the town, Williams College, and other private groups to develop what was then the largest museum of contemporary art in the world, Massachusetts MoCA, in the former textile/Sprague Electric Company mills.

Turn south off Main Street on the Curran Highway for the Heritage State Park, which features various interactive displays about tunnel building and railroading. North off Main Street on Marshall Street leads to the Massachusetts Museum of Contemporary Art. North Adams's Windsor Lake, on the east side of town beyond Massachusetts College of Liberal Arts, is available for public swimming at a nominal fee, as is the pond at Clarksburg State Park, north of the city, beyond Natural Bridge, on Route 8.

WALK

THE CASCADES

1 mile (50 minutes)

North Adams's slightly known treasure is the Cascades. Drive west of town on Route 2; turn left on Marion Avenue, a residential street. If you miss it, turn up Notch Road and take either the first or second left and then right on Marion. Park along the road, being careful not to interfere with private driveways. The trail follows along Notch Brook, first on the east side and then, over a bridge put in by the Berkshire Natural Resources Council, on the west, for .5 mile.

The water tumbles down about 50 feet with a satisfying roar. Although the amount of water varies, generally it is a heavy flow. The folds in the rock that create the falls are worth seeing in themselves. The large hemlocks in the over-story keep the temperature down; the area, virtually in the middle of town, is surprisingly wild and undeveloped. The trail continues on the west side of the brook above the Cascades, really an old woods road, eventually coming out on Reservoir Road. Parts are grown over, however. The Cascades present a fine picnic and cooling off spot.

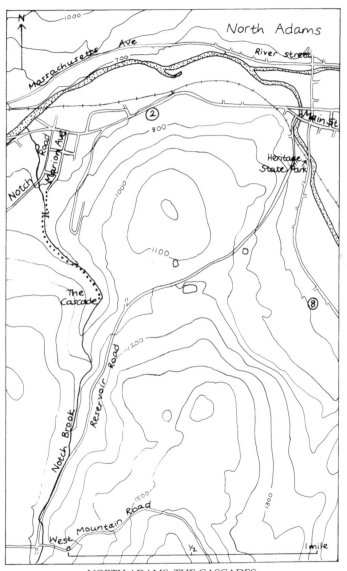

NORTH ADAMS: THE CASCADES

FLORIDA AND SAVOY

In 1753 Captain Elisha Hawley, commander at Fort Massachusetts, then the westernmost wilderness outpost of the Bay Colony and now North Adams, began to build the first road east over the mountains to Charlemont to provision his fort, largely following an Indian route. It climbed to the Western Summit (as it's called now); then followed the line of what is now Central Shaft Road to the Cold River, west of the present Route 2. Samuel Rice, a few years later, built a route closer to the present one, up from Charlemont; for some reason he generally gets all the credit. But then, the auto road called the Mohawk Trail passes through Mahican Indian hunting grounds. The first Savoy settlers, in 1777, called the wet, rocky town, nearly 2,000 feet in elevation, New Seconk, but at its incorporation it was named after a mountainous section of Europe. Florida was incorporated in 1805, at a time when the whole country was excited about a proposed land purchase from Spain. New State Road, by the way, was not named for a construction project by the Commonwealth, but a religious community active in the area in the 19th century.

In those days Savoy and Florida were busy farming and manufacturing towns. You come across many cellar holes, mill sites, and cemeteries, as well as old roads, as you walk. The lack of good farm land and the appeal to go west, especially after the opening of the Erie Canal in 1825, drained this hilly land of its population. On February 9, 1875, the first three flatcar-loads of dignitaries passed beneath Florida, signaling the opening of the Hoosac Tunnel, then the longest in the world (4.75 miles), and more convenient than Hawley's provisioning route. The state purchased a few acres around Borden Mountain in order to erect a fire tower there in 1917, adding 10,000 acres in 1920 to fill out Savoy Mountain State Forest. Construction of the Mohawk Trail led the state to purchase 3,000 acres for the Mohawk Trail State Forest in 1921, the first state campground. Over the years, the state has added more land in

Florida and Savoy to its holdings, so that it now owns fully half of Savoy.

Several CCC units made camp in Savoy in the 1930s. They built many of the dams and the roads, together with stone culverts and bridges. They also planted vast areas of spruce in order to provide for a forestry industry. They built the cabins at South Pond and the picnic facilities at North Pond. Forest HQ is located at a former CCC site. There was a camp at the parking lot at Burnett and New State Roads and one at Tannery Falls. The CCC "boys" must have cursed the black flies in the summer and the snow, which accumulates deeper here than anywhere else in the county, in the winter. In fact, one vicious winter storm nearly flattened one of their bunkrooms.

Road approaches

From North Adams, follow east on Route 2, up around the Hairpin Turn and farther up into Florida. After you pass the Wigwam Gift Shop, bear right at the second turning (5 miles), where a chocolate and white sign directs you to Savoy Mountain State Forest. Bear right at the next two intersections. Both are signed. On your left is the ventilation shaft, originally the central construction shaft, for the Hoosac railroad tunnel, 583 feet below. Hence the name of the road: Central Shaft. Pass forest HQ on the right. Next on the right is the trailhead for the Spruce Hill hike where Old Florida Road enters. Next comes the North Pond parking lot and South Pond camping area. The road, which is in poor shape, changes to gravel. Turn left on Burnett Road. On your left, soon, is an unpaved parking area, the starting point for the stroll to Tannery Falls. Drive right, cross the bridge, and continue south on New State Road. Bear left where Adams Road enters right and then straight where Center Road drops right. You are still on Adams Road, a gravel road now and possibly rough, climbing until a paved road exits right. That is 51 Road, leading up Borden Mountain. In Savoy you drive the gravel roads and hike the paved roads. To reach 51 Road from the south, east, or west, take Route 116 or Route 8A to Savoy Village, then follow Center Road north to Savoy Center, turn right and follow Adams Road to 51 Road on right.

Camping

The Savoy Mountain State Forest camping area is located on South Pond, a mile south of forest HQ on Central Shaft Road. As well as tent and trailer sites (no hookups but toilets and showers), three very popular cabins, used year-round, look out over the pond. Make reservations for state campgrounds by calling 1-877-I-Camp-MA or www.ReserveAmerica.com. The state maintains a campground a few miles east on Route 2, at Mohawk Trail State Forest. Chilson's Pond Campground, north of Route 2 at Whitcomb's Summit, is privately owned. Swimming is available at South Pond, without lifeguards, and North Pond, with lifeguards, for a modest parking fee. Maps of the many hiking and skiing trails are available at the contact station at South Pond.

WALKS

BORDEN MOUNTAIN AND TANNERY FALLS, SAVOY

Various distances

Insects of a biting kind favor this wet, boggy area, so take precautions. They are attracted to perfume and shampoo. For the two strolls on gravel roads sneakers are adequate. Both of these routes are skiable. The strolls can be connected together to make a somewhat wet hiking loop (boots, please) and the roads to make a biking loop.

Park at the end of 51 Road to walk up Borden Mountain. Fifty-one refers to the number of the fire tower the road was built to serve. The climb takes 20 minutes. The trail that bears off to the right partway up makes a loop with Bannis

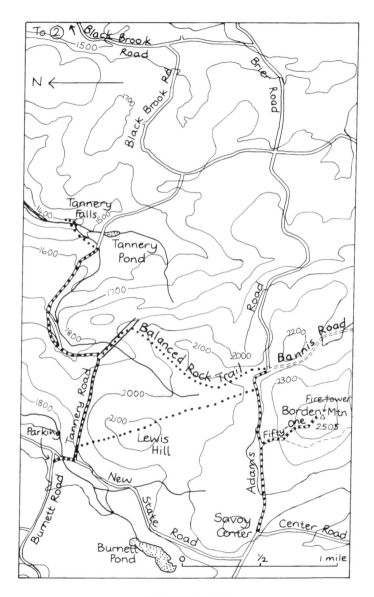

TANNERY FALLS

Road that swings you around Borden Mountain and back to Adams Road; instead, follow straight up the hill to the Walker Lookout Tower—which will likely be locked, because forest fire spotting is apt to be by airplane these days. You can climb the stairs as far as you dare to get above the trees and take in a marvelous view of Greylock, Spruce Hill, and the various undulations of the peneplain (cut-off mountain) that makes up the Hoosacs. Without climbing the tower you won't get much of a view. Your elevation at the top of the tower (2,586 feet) slightly surpasses that of Spruce Hill (2,566). It would be nice to think people wouldn't drop bottles from towers, but apparently the temptation is too much.

You can drive directly to Tannery Falls, either up Black Brook Road from Route 2 at the eastern foot of the Mohawk Trail, or via the gravel Adams or Tannery Roads. On the principle that the value of an experience improves if it is earned, however, park in the dirt lot off Burnett Road near the Gulf Brook bridge. Walk across the bridge and turn left on Tannery Road. (The old road signs in Savoy are nearly illegible.) Simply stay on the road, mostly downhill, for 1.5 miles, about 40 minutes.

You probably won't see a sign for Tannery Falls, but you will see a parking lot on the left. You have gone past it when Tannery Pond appears on your right. Follow the blue blazes from the lot as you work your way down Ross Brook, under wonderful hemlocks. The first falls and chasms in the folded rock are prologue. Follow at the top of the long, delicate falls over a slab of rock. Then, as you work your way to its foot, you discover another brook and falls entering, in season, to the south, and to the right, Parker Brook—the one the CCC dammed to make Tannery Pond. After their union they are Tannery Brook, joining Cold River. Be sure to allow plenty of time to observe the rock, the water, and the trees; read a book or have a picnic here, at least.

Many of the trails in the area are designed for snowmobiling, kept up either by the state or a club, Adams Sno-Drifters. They are not all blazed. Two of these trails connect

Adams Road and Tannery Road, a distance of 1.25 miles each. Park in the lot off Burnett Road, as above, for a 3.5 miles (1.5 hours) walk, starting on Tannery and taking the second right, signed Lewis Hill Trail. Soon you pass an old cemetery. Follow on to Adams Road, east of 51 Road, turning left again in eight minutes on Balanced Rock Trail. You take a left on something more than a trail that soon leads back to Tannery Road. Left again, to Burnett. A pleasant uplands bicycle loop would connect New State, Adams, Black Brook, and Tannery roads: about 8 miles.

HIKE

SPRUCE HILL

Florida and North Adams, 4 miles (1.5 hours hiking time)

Road approaches

Follow directions given under Florida and Savoy up to the trailhead for Spruce Hill hike.

SPRUCE HILL

A relatively short walk over a wide, well-marked although wet trail, this one-trail hike could easily be matched with a picnic at Tannery Falls or a swim at North Pond—or both. The patina derives from lovely, dense, spruce plantations and interesting foundations and stone walls. The last few hundred feet require clambering over some rock. The cliff lookout is not for those who suffer from vertigo. The view, especially west and north, is fine, however.

Walk in Old Florida Road for a few feet before turning right on the Busby Trail, blazed with blue triangles (in state iconography these limit the trail to non-motorized uses). In 2 more minutes, pass beneath the first of two sets of power lines; the second is 11 minutes into the hike. (You'll find good blackberrying in both openings.) Stay left where an

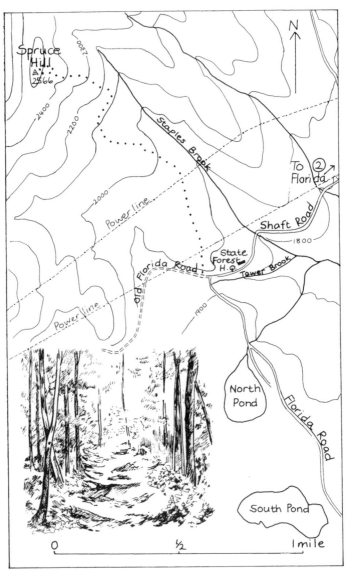

FLORIDA AND SAVOY: SPRUCE HILL

old road enters right. The first part of the trip the trail rises gently on a wide although puddled woods road.

The first evergreens you pass between are hemlock, but soon you come to spruce plantations, planted by the CCC, which had three camps at various locations in Florida and Savoy. You notice Staples Brook on your right. Soon you see where the stream side was walled for a millrun. In fact, Chester Tower owned a mill there in 1855. At 22 minutes you ford a joining brook; the next section of trail is at times indistinguishable from a brook.

At 27 minutes you pass foundations, left, presumably for some sort of a barn, and larger foundations, right, which supported the considerable dwelling. The cellar stones were cut; where the house faced downhill are elaborate terraces, now overgrown, connected by steps. This site appears to have been a farm that by 1904 started taking in summer boarders. It was donated to the Florida-Savoy Land Trust in 1916 and thence to the state. George Busby, however, was granted the right to cross the property to the town road (Central Shaft Road) via the county road (Adams-Florida). Hence the name of the trail.

From here on, the trail rises more steeply. After 5 minutes it crosses through a wall, apparently with a former road on the up side. Soon you reach the first of two steep but brief ascents over rocks. You come out on the outcroppings, looking east, after 45 minutes. You parked your car at 1,900 feet in elevation; this summit rises to 2,566, the highest on the Hoosac plateau (except the tower on Borden Mountain). The view down into the Hoosac Valley and up to the Greylock massif rewards your final burst of effort. The view south, over the Hoosac plateau, is no slouch, either. The trail continues on the summit to other cliffs, where the view of the Green Mountains improves. These cliffs are an excellent vantage point to watch kettles of hawks cavort in the warm air rising from the valley during the fall migration. A short loop returns you to the Busby Trail.

What with taking it easy on the steep sections, it will take you about as long to get down as to climb. If you take the ski option, presumably you park them to climb the last few feet of rocks.

FLORIDA AND MONROE: TUNNEL AND TURBINE

Driving to the trailhead for Dunbar Brook you pass two man-made points of particular interest. The first, in Florida, Massachusetts, is the eastern end of the Hoosac Tunnel. Look left as you cross the railroad tracks. On February 9, 1875, a steam engine first chugged from the Deerfield River Valley to the Hoosic River Valley, in North Adams, through a 4.75-mile-long tunnel, the longest in the world at the time, bored at a cost of 24 years, $15 million, and 195 lives. Discarding an idea dating back to 1825 to surmount the Hoosac Range by canal, those who wanted to join Boston and Albany by this northern route used the best available technology, drilling by hand and blasting with black powder through the rock. Two huge power drills, intended to do the work, both proved incapable; however, an air drill was successfully introduced in 1865. At the same time, George A. Mowbray tried a new explosive called nitroglycerin, a great improvement in blasting but dangerously unstable. A crazy, drunk assistant learned the lucky way that it could be frozen and carried safely. Freight trains still use the line, even though passenger service has long since faded from the northern Berkshire scene.

Florida was a boomtown when the tunnel was under construction, especially the village known as Hoosac Tunnel, at the eastern end. Now you hardly know you are passing through a town. That anything more still exists than a few farms is probably because of the Brookfield Power Bear Swamp pumped storage hydroelectric project in the next town upriver and across the Franklin County line, Monroe. Although several hydroelectric units had existed in the valley previously, the Bear Swamp project was built in the 1970s. The Bear Swamp Visitors' Center, on River Road north of the tunnel, shows an interesting slide-tape on the history of the valley and a working exhibit of pumped storage. Huge, twin pump-turbines generate electricity during peak load periods as water is let out of the Upper Reservoir. The process is reversed, pumping from the Lower Reservoir 770 feet up to the Upper Reservoir, during off-peak times. The penstock that carries the water is 17.5 feet in diameter. Construction of the powerhouse involved removing 97,800 cubic yards of stone.

Road approaches

Go east from Florida, above and east of North Adams on what is known locally as the Trail (the Mohawk Trail, Route 2), take the next left after Whitcomb Summit; then the next right. You head down on a steep road to a T at River Road. The river is the Deerfield. Go left at the T, continuing through the village of Hoosac Tunnel. Soon you pass the Bear Swamp Visitors' Center, right, where you might wish to stop. The parking area you want to find for the Dunbar Brook hike is on the left, .75 mile beyond the visitors' center, 4.5 miles from the Trail.

Camping

You will pass three lean-to (three-sided) shelters, all of which are well maintained (by the state and TransCanada power company), and numerous fireplaces and informal camping areas. A word of caution, though: all the shelters are within a mile of a road and show evidence of being sites for parties. Ideally, shelters should be located a bit off the trail. Using these is like sleeping in the hall. Few services or accommodations are available in Hoosac Tunnel or the next town up, Monroe Bridge, so plan accordingly.

Do not confuse the Spruce Hill hike in Florida with this one on Spruce Mountain in Monroe. Several other spruce hills and mountains exist in the area, for the obvious botanical reason.

HIKE

DUNBAR BROOK

9 miles (4 hours hiking time)

The best is last: a truly scenic walk down Dunbar Brook Trail, beside the tumbling waters of the clear mountain stream, through glades of enormous hemlock, which look as though the underbrush were swept every day. The Commonwealth has declared the Dunbar Valley, like Alander Mountain and the Hopper on Mount Greylock, special Backcountry Areas. This hike suggests alternative routes. Spruce Mountain in Monroe State Forest, Franklin County, is a pleasant hike, not too steep on the south side. There are fine vistas from wire cuts—that is, swaths opened for power lines—and three cliffs along the way. The mountain does not have a cleared summit. A short side trip, partway up, leads to Raycroft Lookout, for a view of the Deerfield Valley. Other links of this loop, all blazed blue, climb up the Dunbar Brook Valley and pass over former and present woods roads. This walk takes you through and near ancient and undisturbed stands of trees, some individuals more than 250 years old. Some are large, but conditions more than age determine size.

The Dunbar picnic area, maintained by TransCanada and the state, is on the east side of River Road. Your trailhead, a smaller parking lot, is directly across from it. Start up to the power line, at the southwest corner of the lot. Above the dam, the trail detaches itself from the jeep road and drops toward the brook, which it follows under spreading hemlock. Look for the blue blazes. Solomon's seal, trilliums, and other spring ephemerals flower in profusion, so that in late May it is impossible to avoid stepping on their beautiful blossoms. After 12 minutes the trail turns left, following close to the river for 4 minutes. You turn up the hill at the trail junction just before the bridge—which you will cross on your return.

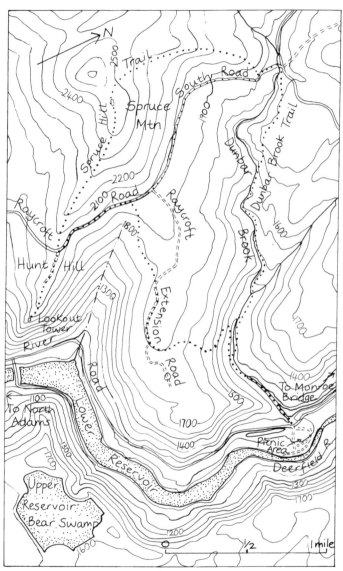

FLORIDA AND MONROE: DUNBAR BROOK

For the next 15 minutes you zigzag up the Dunbar Brook Valley wall. A stone cairn is the sign you are almost at the first shelter; 5 more minutes takes you to Raycroft Extension, a dirt road with large puddles. This is prime mosquito and black fly land; wear your favorite bug repellent. Turn right, following the blue dots. In seven minutes you turn left on a former woods road, somewhat grown in. At 50 minutes from departure you pass the second shelter of the outing, turning sharp right. Straight ahead is deceptively like a path, but actually an intermittent brook bed.

In 55 minutes you pass under a power line you will cross three more times. If the trail has not been bushed recently, it may be hard to spot the opening directly across the cleared area. Ignore extraneous woods roads. Follow the blazes. An hour from the parking lot, you meet South Road. As a check, turning left you should see a cement boundary marker, right. Choices: you can turn right for the quickest way to Dunbar Brook; you can turn left and, in 7 minutes, right, for a 1 hour and 20 minutes jaunt on Spruce Hill; or you can turn left and left again for a 37-minute (times two) visit to the Raycroft lookout tower.

The instructions for Spruce Hill follow. In seven minutes you will cross under those familiar wires, which alert you that you will soon turn. In four more minutes, at an intersection of gravel roads, follow the trail, still blazed blue, right. (Turn left for Raycroft; it's definitely worth it.)

Shortly you pass under those wires, again. This time the cut gives you a nice view of the church spire in Florida. You climb moderately to a plateau, through spruce, oak, and maple, over quartzite outcroppings. In 20 minutes you come to a view, left, over a cliff, of the Hoosac peneplain, the truncated remains of a mountain range. You are in a beech forest. You may think you've reached the summit when the trail begins to descend; but like the boat *Mary Ellen Carter,* it rises again, for about 20 more minutes, to the summit (2,751 feet in elevation; you began at about 1,100 feet). Cliffs to the left show you a view south similar to one you've seen before.

Dunbar Brook

Old mill foundations, Dunbar Brook

Beginning its descent, the trail bends right. At 1:58 you arrive at a trail junction; stay right, still following the blue—which may not be obvious at first. The trail begins to descend sharply, pausing for one more outlook, this time over the hydroelectric project. You pass some beautiful ash specimens before reclaiming the hemlock. At 2:20, turn left on that same South Road you trod before. Look left for some enormous boulders in the woods.

At 2:23 you cross Dunbar Brook on a wooden, automobile bridge. To orient yourself, you may want to follow straight a few hundred feet to the junction with a paved road that leads, as a section called Tilda Road, from the top of the Mohawk Trail and under other names to Monroe Bridge—an alternate driving route. Your trail picks up downstream, just on the north side of the bridge, past some old mill foundations. The brook beckons for swimming or sunning; less public places lie down below.

Thus begins the longest as well as the loveliest leg of the trip, down Dunbar to the car. The trail you are on swings away from the water to join a woods road (2:26), which soon tapers down to a trail through a magnificent hemlock grove.

One thousand needles cushion your every tread. As you descend to the brook, bear right before the large boulder; then zig and zag down. You cross Parsonage Brook, joining from the side on a log bridge . . . and then, yes, once more the wire cut (2:55).

And just six minutes later, the third shelter, where a large brook joins Dunbar, stands right in the trail. Pass behind it, over a bridge. You pass, under continual hemlocks, several informal fireplaces. Seven more minutes bring you to the bridge you saw but did not cross three hours ago. Cross it now. It hangs across Dunbar Brook on two telephone poles. At 3:10, on the south side of the brook now, you come to that turn; 10 minutes more returns you to your car.

Because the dam on Dunbar Brook has a fence across it, don't bother to walk down the path to it.

WALKS FOR THE BLIND
AND DISABLED

by Robert J. Redington

Robert J. Redington lost his sight in 1982. Always an ardent Berkshire hiker, he had an important role in establishing the southern end of the Taconic Skyline Trail (see Long Hikes). Since then he has been working to help blind people enjoy the out-of-doors. Redington describes the following trails for the use of sighted people in assisting the blind to walk in the woods. He suggests that generally the sighted person walk beside the visually handicapped person, explaining any obstacles and also describing the wildlife and views. Where the trail is narrower, the sighted person should walk in front, holding one end of a stick or rope that the blind person also holds with a hand on the same side. A walking stick for the blind person can also be fun and useful. Redington chose relatively smooth trails. The Commonwealth of Massachusetts wishes to cooperate by designating appropriate trails for the blind. In addition, the state has created a wheelchair accessible path, known as Tranquility Trail, at Pittsfield State Forest (for directions see "Pittsfield," this section). Bob Redington graciously allowed us to edit his descriptions for this book.

SOUTH COUNTY

GREAT BARRINGTON AND MONTEREY

WALKS

BEARTOWN STATE FOREST, BENEDICT POND

l.5 miles or more

Road approach

Coming down Route 7 from Stockbridge, turn left just beyond the high school onto Monument Valley Road. Follow it to Stony Brook Road where you turn left. Stony Brook becomes Blue Hill Road. Continue to Beartown State Forest entrance, left. The pond is uphill into the woods. Parking is provided. From Great Barrington, go east on Route 23 to Blue Hill Road in Monterey, turn left, continue past state forest headquarters to the entrance road to the pond.

BENEDICT POND

Beautiful Benedict Pond lies in Beartown State Forest. It is surrounded by woods where mountain laurel bloom in late June and early July. Canada geese are on the pond in the summer. Various hiking routes around the pond can be taken. One, which is nearer the shore with more views of the pond, is the Pond Loop Trail, marked by triangular blue painted blazes and 1.5 miles long. The other route, which is longer and easier walking, follows a road, a woods road (a route with a natural surface and wide enough for a four-wheel vehicle), and a cross-country ski trail. A combination of the two routes can also be followed.

Benedict Pond is the recreation center of Beartown State Forest, with hiking, picnicking, camping, swimming, and, if you bring your own boat—or rent a boat from the concessionaire—canoeing, rowing, and fishing (no motors). A day-use fee is charged per car during the Memorial Day weekend to Labor Day season, but not if the occupants are only going hiking or include a handicapped person suitably identified.

POND LOOP TRAIL

This trail is rough in places, with rocks and roots underfoot and a few steep steps. There are also log bridges and walkways along the trail. These sections call for close guidance by the sighted guide. Hiking is mostly single file along the trail, so the blind hiker and guide should use a guiding stick or rope tether.

The trail starts from the parking area at the Pond Loop Trail sign and blue blaze. Follow it east along the south side of the pond, passing viewpoints at the edge of the pond a few paces to the left of the trail.

The Loop Trail turns left onto the white blazed Appalachian Trail (AT), which it follows at the eastern end of the pond. At a point here you can go left a short distance to a fine vantage point at the edge of the pond.

The trail turns left again on a woods road, and in a few yards the AT goes right while the Loop Trail continues ahead on the woods road, now on the east side of the pond. Next, the trail turns left from the woods road at the sign and follows the northeast and north sides of the pond. Some bog bridging here will require extra care. Finally, the trail turns down the west side of the pond, passing through the campground and ending at a trail sign at the shore of the pond a few yards before the dam at the pond's outlet. There are picnic tables here and a swimming beach nearby.

To complete the circuit back to the parking area, cross on the dam, and go through the picnic area on the wooded knoll to the parking area.

THE LONGER CIRCUIT ROUTE

This route is a mile or so longer than the Loop Trail. It provides smoother walking and is mostly wide enough to permit the blind hiker to walk beside the guide. From the same parking area, take the paved road, which is blocked by a metal gate and has a sign saying, "To the Appalachian Trail." Follow it eastward parallel to the Loop Trail on the south side of the pond. After the AT crosses the road, the pavement ends at a triangular Y junction, where you take the left fork onto the previously mentioned woods road. Soon the combined AT–Pond Loop Trail enters the woods road from the left. Follow the woods road northward on the eastern side of the pond, passing the point where the Loop Trail turns away from it. In another .5 mile, a few yards before the woods road reaches the paved Beartown Road, turn left onto the cross-country ski trail marked by triangular red blazes. Follow this ski trail southwest to the camping area where it crosses the Loop Trail. Turn right on the Loop Trail for the short distance to its end near the dam.

CENTRAL COUNTY

BECKET

NATURE TRAILS

OCTOBER MOUNTAIN STATE FOREST, FINERTY POND

4 miles

Road approaches

From Lee go left (north) off Route 20 on Becket Road, which soon becomes Tyne Road as it enters Becket from Lee. A half-mile from the junction with Route 20, turn left into a woods road and park immediately on the right.

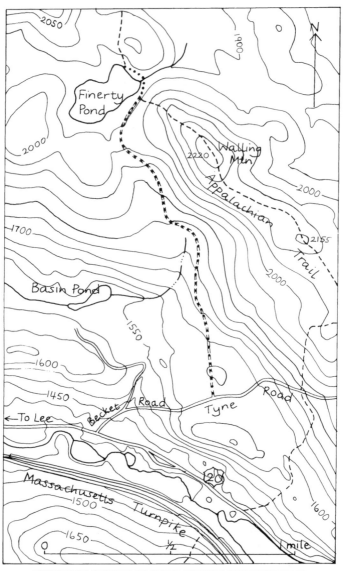

OCTOBER MOUNTAIN STATE FOREST: FINERTY POND

FINERTY POND

Hike north for about 1 mile on the gravel woods road, which is easy walking with a gradual ascent, and reach a junction with a left and right fork. Take the right fork, an old CCC road made with a cobblestone base. There are two rough rocky sections along it, but the route continues to be relatively level. After less than 1 mile on this woods road the AT, with white painted blazes, crosses it. Turn left on the AT, which descends toward nearby Finerty Pond. Soon reach a junction where the AT turns left and an unmarked trail goes right. Continue straight ahead on a faint trail a short distance to the edge of the pond and go a few yards to the right to a large log at the edge of the pond, which is good for several people to sit on. Sighted persons have a good view of the attractive pond from here.

Return to the starting point, retracing your steps over the same route. If you wish to walk farther, when you reach the AT from the edge of the pond, turn left on the unmarked trail and follow it along the southeast side of the pond to the dam at the pond's outlet. There are views over the pond along here. Then retrace your steps. The dam can also be reached by continuing a short way along the woods road beyond the AT crossing, and descending left to the aforementioned unmarked trail to follow it right to the dam.

PITTSFIELD

NATURE TRAILS

PITTSFIELD STATE FOREST

There are two self-guiding interpretive nature trails in the main recreational area of Pittsfield State Forest, an area also containing hiking, ski, and snowmobile trails; picnic areas; campsites; a swimming pond; and a ski jump. A notable feature of the state forest is the Berry Pond area on the crest of the Taconic Range, reached by a one-way, paved circuit road. Here there are splendid views, the largest stand of wild (Pinkster) azaleas in Massachusetts, the highest natural pond in the state (Berry Pond at 2,060 feet), and another self-guiding nature trail especially rewarding for blind persons.

Road approaches

See directions under "Pittsfield, Berry Pond."

TRANQUILITY TRAIL AND WOODS RAMBLE

At the entrance there is a contact station where an attendant collects day-use fees from cars during the late May to early September season. There is no charge if the occupants of a car are to go hiking or include a handicapped person. Just beyond the contact station you can either turn left and drive to the parking area by the ski lodge, which is the access to the two nature trails of the area, or you can drive straight ahead to reach the HQ building and to drive up to the Berry Pond area.

The two self-guiding nature trails, called the Tranquility Trail and the Woods Ramble, start from the same place near the ski lodge. Each one is about .5 mile long, has numbered signposts along it, and makes a loop, which you follow in a counterclockwise direction, keeping to the right where the loop starts. Each trail is wide enough for the blind person to walk beside the guide. The Tranquility Trail is paved, so it may be used by persons in wheelchairs and by those who walk with difficulty. The Woods Ramble Trail is rougher and climbs a way. There are blue painted blazes on part of the trail and on the Hawthorne Trail, which branches off it, so care should be taken to remain on the route with the numbered signposts, shown on the map contained in the Woods Ramble Trail leaflet.

The self-guiding leaflet for each trail, entitled "Nature's Secrets" in the case of the Tranquility Trail, has numbered paragraphs giving information about the plant life and other natural features near the corresponding numbered posts. Each leaflet contains information not provided in the other, and the Wood Ramble leaflet gives additional information of interest concerning the natural history and ecology of Pittsfield State Forest. The two leaflets, as well as the one for the nature trail near Berry Pond, may be obtained from the contact station. The sighted persons can help the blind feel plant life and other natural objects along the trail. If blind persons walking the Tranquility Trail prefer to listen to a recording of the information on the leaflet, they may obtain, at the HQ building, the necessary cassette player and tape.

An additional walk of 1 mile or so to state forest recreational sites may be taken. Start off by walking along the paved road past the ski lodge for some distance. Then turn right on the gravel crossroad, and near its end turn left onto a trail that leads to the ski jump and the swimming pond, formed by a dam in Lulu Brook. You can then either retrace your steps or return via the paved road which passes the HQ building. The walk will also take you past picnic grounds and campsites. You can consult a state forest leaflet and map from the contact station or the HQ building.

BERRY POND AREA

BERKSHIRE HILLS RAMBLE

During the non-snow season, usually mid-April through October, you can drive up the Berry Pond Circuit Road, a one-way route which climbs 1,000 feet to the crest of the range and descends again to the main recreational area. As you reach the crest, look for a broad trail going left from the road where there should be a sign, and where on the right there is a space for two or three cars to park. This is the beginning of the Berkshire Hills Ramble, an interesting, self-guiding nature trail with numbered signposts corresponding to numbered paragraphs on the trail's leaflet. The trail descends somewhat and makes a loop (followed clockwise), which passes the edge of Berry Pond, the distance ending back at the starting point about .75 mile. Blind persons can enjoy the fragrance of the ferns, balsam firs, and the azalea bushes when in blossom, and they can listen to the frogs in the pond.

Drive another .25 mile or so along the road on the crest of the range, past the azalea stands, and park on the right where there is a fine panoramic view over New York State to the west. Then walk up the broad trail to the right of the parking area for a short climb to the top of Berry Hill 2,200 feet in elevation. Here there is a bushy growth and more views. Continue down the other side of the hill, following occasional white trail markers, to the paved road. Turn right to walk back along the road to the parking area. Alternatively, if you did not visit the nature trail on the drive up, you can go a few yards along the road to reach that trail on the left. When you have finished the trail, you walk left on the road for the .25 mile back to the parking area. The walk over Berry Hill and along the paved road, as well as on the nature trail, is the best way to view the azalea bushes when they are in bloom, usually during the first week in June.

If you continue walking along the road past the parking area, you will descend a short distance to Berry Pond on the left. Here an open grassy area gives access to the shore of the pond. You can then follow a broad trail marked with an occasional white painted blaze, which goes between the road and the pond and passes several campsites by the pond. Each one has a picnic table and fireplace. You can then walk back to the parking area and continue driving along the one-way road back down to the main recreational area of the state forest, where the road passes the ski lodge and the access to the two nature trails.

WASHINGTON

WALK

WARNER HILL/APPALACHIAN TRAIL

2 miles

Road approaches

Drive east on Williams Street in Pittsfield, fork left on Kirchner, and make the long climb up the highland to where the AT crosses the road 3.1 miles from the junction below. The trail crossing here is in Washington, where Kirchner becomes Blotz Road, although there is no sign indicating the name change. From the east you can reach the trailhead from Route 8 in Hinsdale, from where it is 1.4 miles along the Blotz/Kirchner side road westward to the trailhead.

Park in the space, if empty, on the north side of Blotz Road where the white blazed AT crosses the road.

WARNER HILL/APPALACHIAN TRAIL

Hike north on the AT, the blind person using a guiding stick or rope tether with the sighted guide. Near the start of the hike pass several fragrant balsam fir trees and cross two muddy spots on stones, if possible. Gradually ascend Warner Hill, passing an extensive stand of red spruce trees and fragrant fern beds. After almost 1 mile, reach the summit of Warner Hill, at 2,050 feet. A short, narrow side trail loops right from the AT to go over the high point of Warner Hill. From this rocky summit there is a view of Pittsfield to the northwest, of the Taconic Range beyond, and of Mount Greylock to the north. Trees have been cut down to open up this view.

Continue north on the AT a short way down from the summit to an extensive stand of fragrant ferns. Before retracing your route to the trailhead, you may wish to hike farther north on the trail, as it gradually descends Warner Hill.

From the trail crossing of Blotz Road, you can hike another .5 mile or so south on the AT. This is pleasant, level walking, past some conifer trees, and you can turn back where the trail starts to climb. There are log walkways over wet places along this trail section.

NORTH COUNTY

ADAMS

MOUNT GREYLOCK STATE RESERVATION, MOUNT PROSPECT

Road approaches

See directions (and information about facilities) under "Adams and Mount Greylock."

MOUNT PROSPECT

This excursion is recommended to last from morning into the afternoon, including lunch. It should be between Memorial Day weekend and mid-October. Generally, the walking is more difficult than on other recommended paths for the handicapped. There are two short, self-guiding nature trails in the Mount Greylock State Reservation. One starts from the east end of the parking lot of the Visitors' Center on Rockwell Road as you begin your drive up the mountain, and the other is located on the mountain range above on the north side of Sperry Road in the public camp-ground. If you wish to visit either trail, or both, ask at the Visitors' Center for the self-guiding leaflet for the trail. At the numbered stops along the trail, the sighted guide can read to the blind person the information in the leaflet describing the plant life and other natural features at these locations.

After visiting the Greylock summit, drive back down to the fork and turn right on Notch Road, which is a continuation north, along the range, of Rockwell Road. You pass on the left open viewpoints westward to the Taconic Range. In 3.5 miles from the fork, park on the right and walk another 100 yards ahead to the AT crossing. Take this trail (white blazes) to the left, passing an open area called Tall Spruces over a rough section of trail. After .5 mile of hiking, reach the Money Brook Trail going left from the AT. Before turning onto this trail, you may wish to continue on the AT another .5 mile or so, ascending to an open section of the crest of Mount Prospect where there is a fine view, northwest, of the Taconic Range and Williamstown. Retrace your steps down the AT and take the Money Brook Trail, now on your right, southwest, through a stand of red spruce trees. The trail is marked with blue state forest markers. After about .3 mile from the junction with the AT, turn right on a red blazed side trail which takes you about 100 yards to the Tall Spruces or Wilbur's Clearing. Back at the Money Brook Trail, you have a choice of routes, as described below.

You can turn left on this trail and retrace your route, turning right at the AT to reach Notch Road and your car. The other choice is to take a longer loop, involving some climbing, by going right farther along the Money Brook Trail. In about a third of a mile, turn left on a side trail with triangular blue painted blazes. As indicated by a sign, this goes to Notch Road on the east. There is a considerable climb up this trail to the road, where you turn left and walk down northward for .5 mile to your car.

APPENDICES
Hikes and Walks by Degree of Difficulty

Hikes and walks are ranked here by a simple system. Walks are rated "A," "B," and "C,"—"A" being the easiest and "C" the most difficult. Hikes are rated "1," "2," and "3," with "1" being the easiest, "2" somewhat more challenging, and "3" the most difficult, mostly based on up and down rather than distance. Where specific distances and/or times are available, these, too, are cited for convenience.

Walk/Hike   **Difficulty/Distance/Time**

SOUTH COUNTY

Mount Washington
  Hikes: Alander and
         Bash Bish Falls 2   7 mi./3 hrs.
         Mount Everett 2   5.5 mi./2.75 hrs.
         Bear Mountain 3   10 mi./4.75 hrs.

Sheffield
  Walks: Salisbury Road . . . . .A   7 mi./2.5 hrs.
         Bartholomew's Cobble/
         Ashley House . . . . .B   approx. 2 hrs.

Egremont
  Walks: Baldwin Hill Road
         North and South . . . . . .A   6 mi./2.5 hrs.
         Jug End C   3 mi./1.25 hrs.

New Marlborough
  Walks: Harmon Road . . . . .A   7 mi./2.75 hrs.
         Campbell Falls . . . . .A   4.5 mi./2 hrs.
         York Pond . . . . .A   1 mile/30 min.

Monterey
Walk: Diane's Trail . . . . .B   1.5 mi./1.25 hrs.

Great Barrington
Walks: River Walk . . . . .A   brief
Seekonk   A   3 or 6 mi./1.5 or
2.5 hrs.
Benedict Pond . . . . .B   1.5 mi./45 min.
Hike: Monument Mountain . .2   3 mi./1.5 hrs.

Tyringham
Walk: Tyringham Cobble . . . . . .B   2 mi./ 1 hr.

Stockbridge
Walks: Ice Glen C   3.5 mi./1.5 hrs.
Bowker's Woods . . . . . . .A   5 mi./15 min.
Prospect Hill . . . . .B   3 mi./1 hr.
Glendale . . . . .B   various
Gould Meadows and
Bullard Woods . . . . .A   various

CENTRAL COUNTY

Lenox
Walks Kennedy Park . . . . .A   3-4 mi./1.5 hrs.
Reservoirs . . . . .B   8 mi. or less/3 hrs.
Hike: Pleasant Valley/
Lenox Mountain 2   3 mi./1.5 hrs.

Richmond
Walks: East Road . . . . .A   4.6 mi./2 hrs.
Stevens Glen . . . . .B   2 mi./45 min.

Chester
Walk: Keystone Arches . . . . .B   3 mi./1.5 hrs.

Peru
Walk: Rice Sanctuary . . . . .B   various

Pittsfield
    Walks: Downtown ....A   8 blocks/30 min.
            Canoe Meadows ....A   various
    Hike: Berry Pond 1   5 mi./2 hrs.

Hancock
    Hike: Shaker Mountain 2   6.5 mi./3 hrs.

Dalton
    Walks: The Boulders ....B   4 mi./2 hrs.
            Wahconah Falls ....A   brief

Windsor
    Walk: Windsor Jambs ....B   3 mi./1.5 hrs.
    Hike: Notchview/Judge's Hill ..1   5.5 mi./2.25 hrs.

NORTH COUNTY

Cheshire
    Walk: Ashuwillticook Trail ....A   3.2 mi./1.25 hrs.

Adams
    Walks: Duval Nature Trail ......A   1.3 mi./35 min.
            Mount Greylock
            Overlook Trail C   2.5 mi./1 hr.
            Campground Trails:
               Stony Ledge ....A   2 mi./50 min.
               March Cataract C   2 mi./45 min.
               Deer Hill C   2.25 mi./1 hr.
            Prospect from
            Notch Road ....B   1 mile/30 min.
            Rounds' Rock ....B   1.25 mi./35 min.
    Hikes: Cheshire Harbor Trail ...2   6.6 mi./2.5 hrs.
            Bellows Pipe Trail 3   4 mi./2 hrs.
                                          (one way)
            The Hopper 2   8 mi./3.5 hrs.
            Stony Ledge and
            Roaring Brook Trails 2   9 mi./3.75 hrs.

Williamstown
  Walks: Mountain Meadow . . . . .B   various
            Stone Hill . . . . .B   1.5 mi./1 hr.
            Sheep Hill . . . . .B   various
  Hikes: Berlin Mountain 3   5.25 mi./3 hrs.
            Pine Cobble and
            Broad Brook Trails 3   10 mi./5 hrs.
            RRR Brooks 2   7.75 mi./3 hrs.
            The Dome 2   6.4 mi./3 hrs.

North Adams
  Walk: The Cascades . . . . .A   1 mile/30 min.

Florida and Savoy
  Walks: Borden Mountain
            and Tannery Falls . . . . . . .B   various
  Hike: Spruce Hill 1   4 mi./1.5 hrs.

Florida and Monroe: Tunnel and Turbine
  Hike: Dunbar Brook 3   9 mi./4 hrs.

LONG HIKES AND TRAIL SYSTEMS

Hikes and Walks in the Berkshire Hills is designed for day trippers, only tangentially describing the long-distance trails in the county. They are well covered in guides specific to them, noted here and in the bibliography. Nor does this book cover more than a fraction of the trails in the county. In particular, many more hikes in northern Berkshire are described in the Williams College Outing Club's guide.

The Appalachian Trail

In the 1920s, Benton McKaye and others used available state-owned land located between convenient small town inns and lodges to plan the Berkshire section of the 2,050-mile footpath from Springer Mountain in Georgia to Mount Katahdin in Maine. It is intended to be a passive, recreational trail. No vehicles are allowed. The 262-mile Long Trail, the length of Vermont, between Massachusetts and the Canadian border, begins on the AT at the Vermont line, north of Pine Cobble.

The more than 86 miles of the AT in Berkshire enter in South County at Sage's Ravine and wander through Mount Everett State Reservation, East Mountain State Forest, Beartown State Forest, October Mountain State Forest, Mount Greylock State Reservation, and Clarksburg State Forest, in the north, exiting the county into Green Mountain National Forest. In recent years, the National Park Service has moved sections in between state forests off roads and onto protected lands, away from the original conception of connecting towns. The AT is blazed with white rectangles, with side trails blazed blue.

Shelters will eventually be placed within a day's hike of each other over the entire length of the trail. Bascom Lodge, on Mount Greylock, is a storied rendezvous for through-hikers, who traditionally received a reduced rate for a night in a real bed, cooked food, and showers by helping in the kitchen. See: *Appalachian Trail Guide— Massachusetts-Connecticut.*

The Mahican Mohawk Trail

The Appalachian Mountain Club, Deerfield River Watershed Association, Friends of Mohawk Trail State Forest, and Hoosic River Watershed Association are laying out a 100-mile trail connecting the Connecticut and Hudson Rivers by following the Deerfield and Hoosic Rivers. Parts have been completed, especially in Franklin County, Massachusetts. The trail is marked by yellow disks with a green maple leaf.

Information is available at the starting point, Historic Deerfield (413-774-5881), or AMC (413-528-6333).

The Taconic Crest Trail

The Taconic Hiking Club, founded in 1932 in Troy, New York, sponsors various kinds of outings. In 1948 its members began to develop the Crest Trail, 29 miles from Berry Pond in Pittsfield State Forest to North Petersburgh, New York. The trail runs generally north and south along a ridge through three states. The Crest Trail is marked by white diamond-shaped markers on a blue square; side trails are marked by blue. As well as Pittsfield State Forest, the TCT runs through New York Department of Environmental Conservation property at Petersburgh Pass, Williams College's Hopkins Forest, and other private land. Once every other year, the club sponsors a one-day, end-to-end hike, beginning with breakfast before dawn at Berry Pond and continuing past dusk. See: *Guide to the Taconic Crest Trail.*

The Taconic Trail System

The entire Taconic system includes the Taconic Crest Trail, the Taconic Skyline Trail, and the South Taconic Trail. The 23-mile-long Skyline Trail runs from Richmond to Williamstown, including the 7-mile section south of Berry

Pond maintained by the Taconic Hiking Club. It follows along the Brodie Mountain extension to the Taconics. About half is in Pittsfield State Forest and half on private land. The blazes are painted white, round or square in shape. The trail is not consistently maintained.

The South Taconic Trail extends 15.7 miles, mostly in New York State's Taconic State Park and Mount Washington State Forest in Massachusetts. It runs parallel to the AT, to the west, and is maintained by volunteers from the New York chapter of the AMC, the Mid-Hudson chapter of the Adirondack Mountain Club, the New York/New Jersey Appalachian Trail Conference, and the Sierra Club. The crest it follows provides almost continuous, open, extensive views east and west, including Alander and Bash Bish (see the description of that hike). Numerous side trails and camping areas provide circuit routes. See: *Guide to the Taconic Trail System.* Hopes have been kindled to connect the two crest trails.

Williams Outing Club Trails

Founded by Albert Hopkins as the Alpine Club in 1863, the Williams Outing Club is the oldest mountain-climbing organization in the United States, preceding both the White Mountain and Appalachian Mountain clubs. Volunteer college students maintain some 75 miles of trails in northern Berkshire, southern Vermont, and adjacent eastern New York. Its trail guide, *The North Berkshire Outdoor Guide,* details trips on some 60 trails in the Williamstown area.

Tour Guides

Greylock Discovery Tours (413-637-4442; 1-800-877-9656; www.greylocktours.com; P.O. Box 2231, Lenox, MA 01240) will guide *group tours* of eight or more along the Appalachian and Taconic Range Trails in half- or whole-day hikes, arranging food, lodging, and cultural events as well. Area newspapers list organized group outings.

BOOTS, BOOKS, MAPS, PACKS

Stores throughout the county sell items useful to hikers; for example, ice cream cones. Nevertheless certain kinds of stores are of particular value.

SPORTING GOODS
South County
Gerry Cosby & Co., 413-229-6600; fax 413-229-3492; www.cosbysports.com; Under Mountain Road, Route 41, Sheffield, MA 01257.

Central County
Arcadian Shop, 413-637-3010; fax 413-637-4112; www.arcadian.com; 91 Pittsfield-Lenox Road, Routes 7 and 20, PO Box 1637, Lenox, MA 01240.

Dave's Sporting Goods, 413-442-2960; 1164 North Street, Pittsfield, MA 01201.

Plaine's Bike Snowboard Ski Shop, 413-499-0294; 55 West Housatonic Street, Route 20, Pittsfield, MA 01201.

North County
Berkshire Outfitters, 413-743-5900; fax 413-743-3359; www.berkshireoutfitters.com; Grove Street, Route 8, Adams, MA 01220.

Goff's Sports, 413-458-3605, 1-800-424-3747; www.williams-shop.com; 15 Spring Street, Williamstown, MA 01267.

The Mountain Goat, 413-458-8445; www.themountaingoat.com; 130 Water Street, Williamstown, MA 01267.

BOOKS

South County

The Bookloft, 413-528-1521; Barrington Plaza, Stockbridge
Road, Route 7, Stockbridge.

Yellow House Books, 413-528-8227; 252 Main Street, Great
Barrington.

Central County

Barnes & Noble, 413-496-9051; Berkshire Crossing Mall,
Route 9, Pittsfield.

The Bookstore, 413-637-3390; 9 Housatonic Street, Lenox.

North County

Papyri Books, 413-662-2099; 45 Eagle Street, North Adams.

Water Street Books, 413-458-8071; 26 Water Street,
Williamstown.

BIBLIOGRAPHY

Appalachian Trail Guide to Massachusetts-Connecticut (1988), P.O. 807, Harpers Ferry, WV 25425-0807.

Binzen, William. *The Berkshires* (a book of photographs) (1986), Globe Pequot Press, Chester, CT.

Brady and White. *Fifty Hikes in Massachusetts* (1983), Countryman Press, P.O. 748, Woodstock, VT 05091.

Burns, Stevens, and Katzelnick. *Most Excellent Majesty: A History of Mount Greylock* (2nd ed., 2009), Berkshire Natural Resources Council, 20 Bank Row, Pittsfield, MA 01201.

Cuyler, Lewis. *Bike Rides in the Berkshire Hills* (1990), Berkshire House, Woodstock, VT.

Drew, Bernard. *A History of Notchview* (1986), Attic Revivals Press, Great Barrington, MA 01230.

Federal Writers Project. *The Berkshire Hills* (1939), reprinted by Northeastern University Press (1987).

Griswold, Whit. *Berkshire Trails for Walking and Ski Touring* (1986), The East Woods Press (out of print).

Ryan, Christopher J. *Guide to the Taconic Trail System* (1989), New England Cartographics, P.O. Box 369, Amherst, MA 01004.

Stevens, Lauren R. *The Berkshire Book: A Complete Guide* (7th edition, 2006), Countryman Press, Woodstock, VT.

Taconic Hiking Club. *Guide to the Taconic Crest Trail* (1988), 810 Church Street, Troy, NY 12180.

Thoreau, Henry David. *A Week on the Concord and Merrimack Rivers* (1893), Houghton Mifflin Co., Boston, MA.

Williams Outing Club. *Northern Berkshire Outdoor Guide* (2008), Williams College, Williamstown, MA 01267.

A Note on the Author

Lauren R. Stevens has lived and walked in Berkshire County for 50 years. He is the author of *The Berkshire Book, Skiing in the Berkshire Hills, Most Excellent Majesty: A History of Mount Greylock* (with Deborah Burns); and *Old Barns in the New World* (with Richard Babcock). In 1982 he founded the *Advocate*, a weekly newspaper. He has also written on outdoor recreation and the environment for most Berkshire publications, and he has published a novel, *The Double Axe* (Scribners). He has served as Executive Director of the Hoosic River Watershed Association. The father of four, Lauren Stevens lives in Stamford, Vermont. He was a professor and Dean of Freshmen at Williams College.